YOU CAN BE A COLUMNIST

Writing & Selling Your Way To Prestige

YOU CAN BE A COLUMNIST

Writing & Selling Your Way To Prestige

Charlotte Digregorio

Civetta Press
PO Box 1043
Portland, OR 97207-1043

Published by: Civetta Press
               P.O. Box 1043
               Portland, OR 97207-1043
               (503) 228-6649

First printing 1993

Library of Congress Catalog Card Number:
90-71020

ISBN: 0-9623318-1-3

Printed and bound in the United States of America

Dedication

This book is dedicated to all the columnists-to-be (hiding out there) who have knowledge and expertise in a professional field or hobby, or those who simply want to share their life's experiences, perspectives, and viewpoints. As you will see, anyone of you is a potential columnist, but this book is for those who dislike anonymity and delight in the recognition they receive from others.

This book is also dedicated to my college students who encourage me to write how-to writing books—what better support system can a teacher have! It's also dedicated to the hundreds of professionals who've taken my workshops and been turned on to the rewards of writing and getting published. (Those last two words are important as you'll learn in this book.)

Further, this book is dedicated to those around me who take the time to talk to me during my writing breaks. Writers always seem to need to bend someone's ear.

Charlotte Digregorio

Acknowledgments

Below, is a list of students who've allowed me to use bits and pieces of their writing to aid as a teaching tool for readers of this book. From these bits and pieces, I was able to expand on their ideas and create columns for instructional purposes. Many thanks to these kind people and gifted writers for their assistance, and best wishes for their continued success as published writers.

Sandy Mulino
Jon Patterson
Edward Klem
Michael Zahn
Joanna Swift
Jan McDowell
Lauren Holtz

Cover by Marcia Barrentine
Interior Design by John Johnson, Media Weavers

Table of Contents

CONSIDER WHO YOU ARE, WHAT YOU KNOW, WHAT YOUR
VIEWS ARE ABOUT LIFE, AND YOU'LL REALIZE THAT YOU HAVE
THE ELEMENTS TO BE A COLUMNIST ◊ HOW TO DEVELOP YOUR
WRITING SKILLS ◊ WHAT A COLUMN REALLY IS ◊ DIFFERENT
ELEMENTS FOUND IN COLUMNS ◊ ARE YOU PREPARED TO BE A
COLUMNIST? ◊ CHOOSING YOUR TYPE OF COLUMN AND
BECOMING SUCCESSFUL

COLUMN STRUCTURE ◊ TYPES OF LEAD SENTENCES ◊ CONTENT:
THE DO'S AND DON'TS ◊ BEING DETAILED ◊ USING DIRECT

STYLE: SIMILES, METAPHORS, ANALOGIES ◊ EFFECTIVE PARTS OF
SPEECH ◊ HYPERBOLE, EPIGRAMS, IRONY, SARCASM

INTRODUCTION

Why I WroteThis Book And How To Use It To Your Advantage

Do you have information to share? Knowledge about some field? Or, ideas and opinions about daily living?

These days, it's often frightening when you consider that we're living in a world where everything is changing daily. We need information and tools to help us to cope: to keep us afloat, to give us the resources we need to succeed financially, to survive daily emotional turmoil, and to keep ourselves physically fit and healthy—to name just a few issues. You probably became increasingly aware of this during the inflationary 80s with changing work and lifestyle patterns, including problems brought on by the need for two-income households. Of course, during the 90s and beyond, we'll need more informational resources as our lives become more complex, and the issues and options in our lives expand.

As our society becomes more complicated and over-credentialed, to compete in the workplace, we also find that there is a glut of professionals in every field, each trying to distinguish himself (herself) and to appear to be the well-known expert, either to attract clientele or to be promoted to a higher position by an employer. Too many law-

13

yers, psychologists, Ph.Ds around—and this list goes on. How can they stand out from the crowd?

If you are a professional, you can stand out from your peers. How? Very simply, by reading this book and becoming a columnist. You need this book if you are ambitious and want to capitalize on your knowledge and expertise and enhance your professional status. Are you an attorney, a physician, investment counselor, psychologist, small business consultant (more entrepreneurs are starting up), accountant, home economist, antique appraiser, dietitian, or someone with other important information to transmit to the public?

An endless variety of professionals will discover the exciting benefits and prestige of being a columnist. Becoming a columnist can not only bring you a larger professional practice and an enhanced image, but it can also unlock rewarding avenues, such as lucrative speaking engagements with associations and civic organizations, and consultations. Talk is definitely not cheap! (It's staggering to hear about the hourly fees speakers and consultants command today.)

Quite simply, as a columnist, you'll become recognized as an expert in your field. Your photo and name, regularly seen in one or more publications, can bring you great exposure, credibility, and financial enrichment. You don't have to be the best in your field to be a columnist—just competent and knowledgeable. (Keep this in mind and go for it.)

Or, if you have an interesting hobby to share, you, too, can enjoy the recognition and excitement of being a columnist. Are you an avid traveler, a dedicated stamp collector, a good cook?

And, what if you're a homemaker or a retiree and you want to be columnist? Let's take the homemaker. You have valuable information to share. Besides the joys and the hardships of raising kids (which make for good reading in themselves), what have you learned about running a household and raising kids—tips you can share to make the journey a little less bumpy for other moms? Other homemakers need your knowledge or sharing of perspectives.

You're not Erma Bombeck, you're thinking? That doesn't matter. You don't have to be. Be an innovator! Be different than Bombeck. That's the key! There is plenty of room for new angles and new ways of expressing oneself on running a household and parenthood. Bombeck has one style. You have another. And, your different style or fresh approach just may appeal to the public.

You may even become more popular than Bombeck. It's possible. Stand up and be counted. Don't be afraid to tell everyone you are a writer—a columnist—even if you haven't yet been published. Start believing in yourself. Visualize your success and you will be a published and successful columnist. Stop comparing yourself to famous columnists and thinking, "I'm not as good as them."

What if you're a retiree? You have interesting perspectives, too—about marriage, divorce, raising kids. Nostalgia is in, too, as people like to read about how life has changed.

Whoever you are, you possess information or insights about some subject which are marketable. This book will help you get your ideas out and running on paper and will help you consider what areas of your expertise you'd like to offer to the public.

You may not have even realized that you have a special expertise. You will, with this book. And, this book will also help you open your mind to discover topics within your base of expertise to write about.

Of course, this book will instruct you in basic journalistic style so that your work will be acceptable to editors, instead of being discarded in the stack of poor or hackneyed freelance writing submissions. Most everyone has knowledge or insights to share, but you can't attract an editor to consider your columns unless they conform to some basic journalism standards.

Of equal importance, this book will instruct you on a step-by-step basis on how to sell your work, beginning with the small markets and working up to the larger ones, so that if you desire, someday you may be able to crack the syndication market. Yes, it's a gradual process. After all, in the job world, you don't start out at the top as president of the company. Likewise, as a columnist, it is unlikely that you would start out being carried by a syndicate unless you had some influential contact there.

Year to year, from my teaching experience, I can't even count all the aspiring columnists out there who never got published simply because they didn't know how to market what they wrote (or they didn't want to take the time to do it).

Simply put, getting published involves selling what you write, and don't ever forget this. I repeat, don't ever forget this!

As for reading this book, don't skip any chapters. I've included chapters on how to write a "creative" column (insights on daily life) and an informational column (about hobbies and professional areas). If you are now considering writing a creative column, don't skip the chapter on writing an informational column and vice versa. After reading these chapters, you may just change your mind about the type of column you'd like to write. More importantly, you'll pick up ideas from both chapters that you can apply to whatever kind of column you're writing.

Use this book as a workbook. Underline the text and take notes in the margins for maximum assimilation. Yes, just like you did when you were a student. Although I don't think you'll find this book to be drudgery—just a light, lively tutorial. In particular, carefully study the sample columns along with the commentaries which follow each of them. Further, do not forget to read the appendix where valuable reference books and directories are listed which will lead you to select publications where you can submit your columns. The appendix also includes syndicated columnists' anthologies. You must read the latter to catch on to how columns are written and their unique style. In addition, the appendix also includes books on journalistic writing style and writers' magazines which will also help you develop your columnist style. Read, read,

read—especially columns written by others. Force yourself to, if you're not a constant reader.

One last note: you'll notice that I often use the pronoun "he" throughout this book. This often offends readers, perhaps some who appear to be on the prowl for these examples of "inequality." As a writer (and human being) , I think that too much is made about the need to avoid the exclusive use of the masculine pronoun. I even think that too many books have been written about gender usage in writing. I hope that readers will focus their efforts on profiting from the information in this book, rather than being sidetracked by the gender issue.

Chapter 1

BE A COLUMNIST!

If you've read the introduction of this book (and you should have) you know by now that whoever you are, regardless of your background, interests, or education, you can be a columnist. That's a fact! You can, for example, be a columnist by drawing from your professional expertise, from your expertise as a hobbyist, or merely by drawing from life's experiences or perspectives.

Everyone knows this is the Information Age and people are interested in information or ideas which instruct them or help them to solve their problems. You can cash in on your know-how. No, you don't have to be a world-famous authority in your field, just as long as you have information which others need and that they can gain from. So what if another professional or hobbyist knows more than you do? You have just as much a right to offer your information to the public as he does. As a knowledgeable professional or hobbyist in a certain field, you don't even have to be among the best in your field to be a columnist. What it boils down to is, do you know your field better than most people who will be reading your column? Not all people, but most people? Then you can be a columnist!

You can also be a columnist by drawing from your daily experiences or thoughts. Take the homemaker. You may already know that Abigail Van Buren of "Dear Abby" and Ann Landers were housewives who entered newspaper contests to become columnists. They won the contests, and after their columns ran in their local papers, they received a lot of exposure and were offered syndication.

To be a columnist, you don't need to be a professional writer, nor even have a writing background. However, to set your work apart from the poorly-written freelance material that most newsletter, newspaper, and magazine editors receive (and throw out), you need to know some basic journalistic skills. Further, you need to know how, when, and where to approach editors with your work.

You don't even have to be a regular columnist, writing weekly, biweekly, or monthly. You may just want to submit a guest column to a publication or publications from time to time, thereby getting some exposure and recognition.

Whatever your goals as far as frequency of published columns, you must get the system of writing journalistically and selling to publications down pat.

In the 90s, there will be increasing need for columnists, particularly those who have expertise in professional fields and who can explain often complicated subject matter to the layperson.

Are you a nurse? Why not write a regular column on caring for the elderly who are becoming an ever-larger segment of our society?

Are you a teacher? Maybe you'd like to write a regular column which deals with topics such as how parents should handle their kids and discipline them. Or maybe your topics could include how parents can help further their children's academic success, deal with school problems, or communicate with teachers. Look for major issues in your field. Consider your conversations with parents and what concerns they've voiced, for example. Discipline and academic achievement are just a few of them.

You must also decide if you want to write columns for

your peers, thereby targeting an academic newsletter or trade magazine, or for a newspaper, thereby targeting the general public.

Are you a counselor or social worker? So many people these days suffer from problems such as addictions—alcohol and drugs are just a few out of dozens. Why not write columns to help people learn self-help skills to cope with problems?

Are you an author with an expertise on particular topics such as cooking or travel? Why not spin off columns from your books, going into greater detail on a particular topic which you might have mentioned in passing? As an author, a major benefit of being a columnist is that your credit line at the end of each column could include mention that you are the author of a particular book. Inevitably, sales of your book will greatly increase with this added exposure.

About getting columns published, you've probably read local columnists in your community paper or even syndicated columnists who write poorly and who can't explain information well. Sure, they've gotten published anyway. How? They probably had connections at the publication or at the syndicate. Or, maybe they previously wrote a book (edited by a good writer) which established them as an authority in their field. Or, maybe they are famous personalities on radio or television.

If you're a poor writer and don't have connections, you're probably out of luck as far as being a columnist.

However, if you learn the skills in this book, you won't need to rely on connections. You'll be able to write in a way that is presentable to editors, and you'll also discover how, when, and where to effectively deal with editors. You can get your break as a published columnist.

Let me tell you a little bit about my background. I didn't start out as a journalist. After getting out of graduate school with degrees in foreign languages, I taught foreign languages for a brief time. Afterwards, I reassessed my situation and decided I wanted to go into a different field. At first, I didn't know what field I wanted to pursue, so I asked myself what general kinds of things I liked to do best. The answer I came up with was that I liked to read, learn about all kinds of topics, write letters, and talk to people. Although these interests didn't seem to add up to anything specific in the job world, broadly, I came up with a possible link: journalism.

In fact, I did pursue journalism. I started out at entry level positions in the journalism field and was employed through the years at a myriad of publications. For example, I was a feature editor, and later a columnist on community issues at a daily newspaper. As a feature editor, among other duties, I edited freelance columnists' work for my lifestyle section of the newspaper. The variety of freelance columnists who worked for me through the years was large: a horticulturist writing a gardening column; an economics professor writing about his hobby of wine tasting; a psychologist writing a self-help column; a social worker writing a family life column; a home economist writing a cooking column; and a homemaker writing a column on daily living—marriage and child rearing.

Through the years, I've also taught journalism at two and four-year colleges and universities, along with teaching non-credit adult workshops throughout the country which have included those on how to be a columnist. I decided to teach workshops on how to become a columnist due to my prior experience of having edited freelance columnists' work as a feature editor. I realized that no matter what type of column I edited, written by a non-trained journalist, the column contained the same basic writing mistakes. In general—we'll get into the specifics later on—non-journalistically trained people write in English composition style, which is not only frowned upon by editors, but it just doesn't appeal to readers of publications who expect to be grabbed by a snappy, crisp style.

It's only natural that people who aren't journalists don't write in a way which adheres to the unique language, form, and structure of journalistic writing. When I was growing up, as when you were, I learned the English composition style in school—often one of turgidity, wordiness, repetition of key points, and building up to key points. That doesn't work as a journalist. You must learn to make your points succinctly and do it early on in your piece.

I started from scratch and learned journalism basics and you can, too. It's simple to catch on to the style, especially if you read famous syndicated columnists on a regular basis in any daily metropolitan newspaper.

Once you do learn the journalistic style, you must not accumulate a stack of columns and leave them sitting in your desk drawer, never to be seen or read by others. Oh, the number of adult workshop students I see each year who have let their columns turn yellow! Out of frustration, they enroll in my class, not having the foggiest of how to market their columns.

Consider this book to be a workshop in itself, without your having to invest workshop time or money. You will learn specifically how publications are structured with the hierarchy of editors—which to approach so you'll be able to attack the newsletter, newspaper, and magazine markets with success. There are thousands of publications which you can become familiar with if you read through some of the directories which I've listed in the appendix of this book. After perusing these first, before you launch into writing and marketing, you will be able to decide if you want to target newspapers, magazines, or newsletters, and whether you wish to write for professional or trade publications or general interest publications to relay your material to its deserving audience. These directories specifically describe publications and their circulation size so you'll, in turn, be able to target your specific audience. Now it's important to take the attitude that what you write will benefit your readers, your deserving audience, and that they'll be grateful for your writing.

In this book, you'll be exposed to a variety of columns, both good and bad, and I'll be commenting on each of them. Therefore, no matter what kind of column you choose to write, you'll have a clear concept of how columns should be written. In short—the do's and don'ts of column writing. You'll also find helpful examples of good and bad writing techniques pertaining to the journalism style, in general.

If you want to develop your skills as a columnist, in your spare time, you should be reading columns. The simplest and most complete way of doing this is to check out anthologies of columnists' work at your local library. I have listed my choice of anthologies in the appendix of this book. Almost all of the anthologies listed and described are those of syndicated columnists and they represent a variety of writing styles and subject matter. Read them in the bathroom, especially in the bathroom, since columns are short little takes which can be read quickly. Make them a part of your bathroom library.

A lot of syndicated columnists are on newspaper staffs. Among the syndicated columnists in the appendix are Anna Quindlen, columnist of *The New York Times*. In the past, she wrote about daily living and perspectives on different aspects of her life. Her book, *Living Out Loud,* is a compilation of those columns. (Currently, she writes a column which focuses on issues in the news.)

Among other columnists' work in the appendix, are Erma Bombeck's anthologies, and I'm sure most of you have often read her columns. Whether or not you like Bombeck's impressions of daily living, she is a skilled writer with a crisp, concise journalistic style, and one who undoubtedly knows how to write with humor.

Also mentioned in the appendix are Russell Baker, columnist of *The New York Times*, and Bob Greene of *The Chicago Tribune*. Baker tends to appeal to the educated upper middle class and he often writes about his perspectives on daily living. Greene has an unmistakable style, writing about topics which practically everyone can relate to, and he often formulates his columns after observing and interviewing the "common man" types. Greene writes columns, therefore, in the typical reporter's style, often along the creative column lines. At times, Greene interviews celebrities and builds columns around them, analyzing why they are popular with the general public. Greene's columns are very enjoyable.

Still other columnists in the appendix are Mike Royko, staffer of *The Chicago Tribune* , unmistakable for his outspokenness and sarcasm on political issues. You are probably also familiar with Ellen Goodman, staffer of the *Boston Globe*. She writes with much depth, often on pressing women's issues. Whether you agree with her ideas or not, her columns are worthwhile to read due to her methodic and logical arguments, and for the adept way she builds her arguments. Also, I highly recommend syndicated columnist Roger Simon whom I used to read frequently when he was at *The Chicago Tribune*. He writes with much clarity and wit on politics, and yet his style is not the abrasive one which Royko sometimes demonstrates.

Of course, read your local newspapers, not only the large metropolitan ones which carry the syndicated columnists, but also your weekly community papers. If you decide to write a hobby or professional type of column, begin by seeing what others in your area are writing about. Afterwards, expand your research to publications outside your area, such as metropolitan papers in other parts of the country. Of course, these can be found at your local library or at a local newsstand. In so doing, your goal will be to see what others are writing about and to offer the public something fresh, or even a new angle on a common type of column.

If you're writing for peers in your field of expertise, see what trade publications in various parts of the country are running.

Considering What A Column Really Is

I'm sure you picked up this book having some idea of what a column is. Let's review the basics. As you know, a column can be identified by its byline. (Byline means "by" plus the writer's name as in "By Mike Royko.") Often, there's also a sketch or photo of the columnist. However, this is sometimes left out if space considerations are a factor. Further, the column is identified by a regular heading (logo). For example, when I was a feature editor, I had a freelance columnist who wrote a wine tasting column for my section of the newspaper which he called "The Grape Vine." As you see, many times the column's logo is a play on words. (You should come up with a possible logo for your column before you approach an editor with a few sample columns. We'll discuss this more, later in the book.)

Whether you're writing for a newsletter, newspaper, or a magazine, your particular column, if it's a regular feature, usually runs on the same page each time, or at least in the same section, so readers can easily find it on the particular day when it's scheduled to run. After all, it's a fact that some readers buy a publication solely to read their favorite columnist, and they turn immediately to the column.

A column, unlike a news article, for example, must be subjective by its very nature, biased with the writer's opinion. It is written in the first person, and it carries a point of view or moral to it. A column not only states an opinion on the writer's perspective on certain information, but it should do so in an interesting, entertaining, and readable way. Sadly, many columnists out there neglect these basics. All these particular columnists seem to accomplish is to crank out a column, not caring about its quality—just getting it in print. It's become nothing more than an obligation.

Types of columns are as varied as the imagination. There are columns from pet care and stamp collecting, to columns on how to invest your money. Obviously, if you want to write for general interest (general audience) publications, then the type of column you should write is one that would appeal to a large segment of the general population.

There is always room for new ideas for columns. In fact, the new ideas are those which sell especially well. However, you can also have a fresh angle on a commonly-written about subject. In the latter case, it should be a really fresh angle to attract an editor.

Typical columns include: humorous columns on daily living; advice columns like that of Ann Landers; political or public affairs columns on current events and issues; sports columns (though these are usually written by a publication's staff writer); and self-help columns. The latter have been the trend of the 80s, and I'm sure they will continue to be popular in the 90s and into the 21st century.

Social critic columns on the American way of life (trends and values), such as the ones Russell Baker writes, are also popular. Baker deals a lot with urban life. Conversely, in your own backyard, if you live in suburbia or in a small town, you could write columns on small-town American life, and they could be popular as more people exit the large cities. Popular, too, are the localized society columns on personalities and events, such as the ones you find in the weekly papers. The latter owe much of their success to the fact that they include gossipy tidbits, so you would have to feel comfortable with offering a certain amount of gossip if you were to succeed in this realm.

Today, bylined columns appear everywhere in a publication—in every section of your local newspaper. When I look through my local metropolitan newspaper, it seems as if it's a newspaper filled with too many columns. Although I love reading columns—and that's one reason I wrote this book—perhaps much of this column space in newspapers should instead be devoted to more news articles with objective reporting, rather than opinions. Columns sprinkled here and there are great, and they are appreciated by readers. However, too many spoil the very nature of the news business. Readers often need more factual information which news articles offer, so they can form their own opinions. (So much for my mini-column on columns!)

In the early 20th century, bylined columns were an adjunct to the newspaper editorial page. Today, one can clearly see the popularity of columns since they've extended to virtually every section of most newspapers. This may point to the fact, for example, that people in modern society have often become more lonely and alienated due to divorce and broken families. And, we feel, in general, isolation in the big cities, as well as in the suburbs. Too, more and more people work in their homes, sometimes feeling removed from "life." People in these situations tend to look for human contact which they can find in columnists they regularly read in their local newspaper. These columnists are vicarious friends who give them advice on personal or professional matters in this ever-complicated world. They alleviate people's fears and concerns. Given these factors, there is a growing need for columns.

Different Elements Found In Columns

Below, I've listed some typical elements found in columns. Of course, it's important to note that not all columns have every single one of these elements. It obviously depends on the type of column you write and the style you feel comfortable using.

For example, not a lot of people would feel comfortable writing in Mike Royko's irreverent, biting style, but it's a possibility for some of you, and maybe this style would turn out to be a good selling point for you. (Just be careful not to libel anyone. See the appendix for *The Writer's Friendly Legal Guide*).

The first 10 elements are essential to practically any column.

1) **Opinion and/or Advice.** These are the foundation of all columns.

2) **Information.** Obviously, all journalistic pieces, columns included, need this.

3) **Use of Examples to Support the Information.** All columnists should support their information with examples, rather than just make blanket statements.

4) **Logic.** All arguments should be stated in a logical way.

5) **Thought-Provoking Statements/Insights.** You must give readers food for thought and let them see some

issue in a different light from how they may have originally viewed it.

6) **Entertainment/Conversational Style.** The former could involve using anecdotes, or even the telling a story as an example of an analogous situation. The latter could include dialogue, such as recreating a conversation you had with another person. Or, it could involve fabricating a conversation in order to illustrate your point, as is often done in humorous columns, such as in those of Mike Royko and Erma Bombeck.

7) **Observation.** In order for a columnist to come up with ideas to write about, he must observe certain situations. In his writing, he will include those observations.

8) **Analogies/Comparisons.** These are basic journalistic style tools. Journalists, no matter what kind of piece they're writing, should include analogies and comparisons so that readers can readily grasp their point.

> Example of Analogy: When you go to traffic court for your speeding ticket, you have to watch a film on safe driving. This makes you feel like you were back in high school taking a driver's education course.

Similes create a likeness between two things by including the word "like" or "as" between the two.

> Example of Simile: Her passport photo made her look like a prison inmate.

Metaphors, for example, suggest a resemblance between two things which are totally unrelated, and furthermore, the claim is literally impossible.

> Example of Metaphor: The rock singers were wild animals.

Syndicated columnist Erma Bombeck is very adept at creating interesting, humorous similes and metaphors. However, realize that besides using similes, metaphors, and all kinds of comparisons in humorous columns, these devices are also very helpful in serious informational columns. For example, draw analogous situations whenever you can to facilitate an explanation. Of course, make certain that these analogies are ones which can be easily understood by the reader. Let me give you an example. Have you ever, to your frustration, sat in a lawyer's office and listened to an analogy, which, in fact, you couldn't follow? My point is, don't ever leave your reader confused by an analogy which was supposed to clarify the information. (When, in doubt, have a person unfamiliar with that type of information read your column to see if it makes sense to the layperson.)

9) **Liveliness.** Even a business, religious, or legal column can be lively with colorful verbs and adjectives, in addition to analogies and interesting observations. Besides avoiding over-used verbs and adjectives, you can achieve liveliness through alliteration of verbs and adjectives (repetition of their initial consonant sounds).

> Example of Alliteration: His investment advice left me befuddled, beleaguered, and bereft of my savings. (Note: the alliteration is achieved through the b's.)

10) **Briskness.** Don't drag on and on, repeating your point mercilessly, in different ways. All journalistic writing, whether news reporting or column writing, involves making your point without redundancy. Briskness also means keeping your sentences short and crisp, as journalists consistently strive to do. And, if you use dialogue, keep it moving, with short, punchy statements.

11) **Paradox.** This is a statement which seems contradictory, but which can be true. Columnists often use this for comic effect.

> Example: He lives in a palatial shack.

12) **Humor/Wit**

- Irony—Saying the opposite of what is meant by re-lying on context to indicate one's meaning. For ex-ample, a column written about how lawsuits have become excessive might include the statements: "The world is a friendly place. Don't leave home without a lawyer."

- Sarcasm—A cutting, biting remark against some-one. Example: City Council members probably can't even balance their own checkbooks.

- Satire—Irony or sarcasm which ridicules human na-ture and vices. Example: The landlord demon-strated his philanthropy by renting rooms to indigents for half the regular rate, provided they would share quarters with roaches.

- Hyperbole—An expression of gross exaggeration of a point for the effect of mockery. (Syndicated col-umnists Roger Simon, Mike Royko, and Art Buchwald are adept at hyperbole.) Example: After eating one slice of blueberry cheesecake, he went into a stupor.

- Parody—A ridiculous imitation/caricature. Ex-ample: The wealthy old codger was so overweight that before he approached the dining room table, the butler pushed together twenty chairs.

- Irreverence—Some of Mike Royko's columns are a classic example of this, as he openly uses insulting words against people. However, keep in mind that cheap shots should not be taken at others. Royko is fair, as any columnist should be. Only bad col-umnists write to get back at people. It's acceptable to blast someone in a column for something that was deserved, but make sure your motives have nothing to do with revenge or malice. As a colum-nist, you must always be honorable in that it is your purpose to inform and aid the public in be-coming more aware of some topic. Caution: under this category of "irreverence," be careful not to get involved in libel. Anyone can sue for anything these days, whether or not their case is frivolous. Even frivolous cases against a writer run up a legal bill. Incidentally, liability insurance for writers is prohibitively expensive—if you can even find an insurance company to insure you. (Remember, a good book to read which includes discussion about libel is *The Writer's Friendly Legal Guide*, edited by Kirk Polking.) Often, columnists who use insults or even criticize the character of someone, tread the fine line of libel, even though opinion is commonly protected in the courts. Be sure of your ground, if you choose to undertake the route of irreverence.

Final Note On Different Elements Found In Columns

Whichever elements of style you choose to use, don't forget that your advice or arguments need to be strong, particularly if you are writing about an issue. You also must be fair by offering your reader information about opposing viewpoints. You always have to anticipate the arguments of your opponents and address them, too. Caution: even if a few of your arguments and the opposing arguments are those which practically everyone has heard about before in the news, you have to bring them up anyway, to show that you've considered them and also to inform the few readers who may not have heard them before. Of course, bring to light new arguments or perspectives, too.

Are You Prepared To Be A Columnist?

If you develop the traits and skills described in this section, you can become a good columnist. Remember, no one says you have to be as good a columnist as syndicated journalists Ellen Goodman or Roger Simon. And, of course, also consider that many syndicated columnists you've read—particularly those written by non-professional writers imparting information in a certain field—are bad ones. My point is, you can learn to do an adequate and good job, writing well and presenting your ideas and/or information in an interesting way.

What is required of you?

• **Energy/Discipline/Commitment.** You'll have to crank out a column on a regular basis, unless you choose to be a guest columnist writing at your leisure, for various publications when the opportunity arises. As a regular columnist, how often you have to submit a column largely depends on the particular publication's frequency of circulation, and the editor's needs. It may be four columns, or just two, or one column a month. Or, if you write for a quarterly newsletter, you may just be writing four columns a year. Of course, you can negotiate the arrangement. Be conservative. Don't commit yourself to writing more than you can effectively do well, given your schedule and other commitments. Too many columnists write bad columns here and there when their schedule gets too hectic. Each one of your columns must be good if you are to survive as a columnist over a period of time. Realize that the public is fickle and impatient, so even one bad column, and a lot of readers might drop you.

You need discipline in sitting down to write and sticking to a writing schedule. You can't just dash off a column at the last minute. Even professional writers find that writing columns requires a lot of work. A lot of syndicated columnists who are professional journalists on staff at publications spend an entire day writing and perfecting a column, including verifying information. They may take even longer if it requires researching information, including going over news articles written by other journalists on the issue.

You must be willing to commit yourself for a certain period of time, even though as a beginning columnist, rarely would you be signing any contracts with editors. Realize that editors will probably not want to commit themselves. You'll most likely be given a trial period of a few months to see if your column is catching on. Even after that, a contract would be very rare.

You need the momentum to sustain your efforts. Can you make the commitment to write a column over a year's period? You'll have to make an informal commitment, even if there is no contract. Do you have the spare time?

• **Imagination or Enterprise.** If you don't have both of these, you must have one of them so that you can come up with ideas to write about.

• **Be Reflective.** You must be reflective and methodical to define your ideas and opinions well, first in your mind and then on paper. You don't need to make an outline, unless you feel comfortable doing one. I rarely meet a journalist who writes outlines. Personally, I feel notes are adequate to write from.

• **Always Record Thoughts/Ideas/Observations.** That's right. Always. Wherever you are, wherever you go, tote a notebook, as most all professional writers do—18 hours a day. If you're writing a creative column, record your likes, dislikes, diversions, pet peeves, thoughts on human nature, daily living, and past experiences you've learned from.

Ideas and thoughts are coming to you by the thousands every day, many of them not directly related to your column, but others of them are. As ideas come to you which you feel may perhaps be significant to your writing, jot them down. You'll begin to spot common themes in your observations which you can build columns around. If you're writing an informational column from your professional or hobbyist expertise, also carry a notebook. During your workday (or even during your day of leisure) you'll be exposed to ideas or information which you can integrate into your column.

It's true that a lot of professional writers even keep a notebook and pencil by their bed in case they wake up during the night with an idea. Keep one there and also one in your car and one in your pocket. I do. Then keep your eyes and ears open. There's an idea for a column in practically any situation, whether you're writing creatively about daily life or about your profession or hobby.

Start thinking like a journalist. Any good journalist realizes that ideas to write about are everywhere if only you stop to look, listen, observe, and analyze a situation. Don't take anything for granted. Whatever you see, hear, feel, touch, smell, record it!

• **Be Perceptive.** Do what Erma Bombeck does. She recognizes a common experience or problem in daily life and writes about it. Even if you're writing a serious, informational column, such as a legal advice one, recognize common legal problems which people face, and which they need answers to. As a professional in your field, draw general ideas from your own practice with clients. Just like my students give me writing ideas, your clients also offer a fountain of ideas.

• **Be Curious.** Keep informing yourself about your area of expertise if you are writing a column on professional or hobbyist matters. If you're writing a creative column, be curious about life. Analyze it. If you're writing the latter, analyze trends in life and how others feel about them.

Being curious involves learning new things, through attending lectures, seminars, workshops, association meetings (the latter, especially if you're a professional and they are relevant to your field). Also attend luncheons with interesting speakers on a professional topic, or even on just a topic about living well.

• **Keep a Current File of Clipped News Articles.** These provide column ideas. Inspiration is everywhere, from tabloids like *The National Enquirer* to trade journals, depending on your particular type of column writing interests.

• **Cultivate Sources.** Keep an index file of names and phone numbers of professional people, friends, and relatives who can provide you with expert information or interesting ideas about a topic which may come up in your writing. Ann Landers and other advice columnists seem to have an endless reservoir of professional sources. Whenever you meet people, whoever they are, always ask for their business card. Who knows when you may need to call on them for something.

In writing an informational column, for example, you may even need people to consult with if you are not a specialist on a particular subject within your field or a related field. As a columnist, don't forget that you've become well-known, maybe even a celebrity of sorts. Therefore, you can even make cold calls to professional people in the phone book that you don't know, and they'll be flattered to be quoted in your next column. Others will be happy to oblige you, because they'll be getting exposure for themselves at the same time. When I was a columnist, on staff at a newspaper, like a typical journalist, I was always calling up people I didn't know for information, such as professor-experts in a certain field at the local university. If a person wasn't in his office at the time of my call, I'd leave a message with a receptionist or a secretary, saying that I was a columnist for such and such a publication and that I needed a few comments to quote him on. In these cases, no one ever failed to call me back.

If you write a column on politics, for example, you not only need to cultivate a broad knowledge of politics, but you need to cultivate politicians as sources for inside information or secondary information which you don't have.

If you're writing a creative column on your perspectives on daily living, you don't always need inside sources for information. However, once in a while, you may need quotes or comments from professionals in various fields to supplement your own opinions, perspectives, or ideas about life.

Whatever your type of column, you need to talk to a lot of people. Meet people in different situations, go out and observe people. For example, if you are a homemaker writing a column on daily living, go out and talk to other parents at PTA meetings. If you are a single person writing a singles column, talk to people at a church group for singles or attend Parents Without Partners' meetings. Keep your pulse on what's happening and how other singles think. Listen to what issues are on their minds.

Furthermore, make a point of asking your friends, relatives, and neighbors who they know who is interesting. They may tell you about someone who'll be mentioned in your next column—or someone who'll even be the subject of your next column. Let people know that you are looking for ideas to write about. Never be bashful in asking for help in this way.

As a columnist, you'll quickly become a social type of person, even if you weren't previously. By necessity, you'll constantly be talking to a lot of people who will fuel your thoughts and ideas about a variety of subjects. You'll even be talking to readers who are strangers, if you desire to contact them after they've written to you in care of the publication(s) your column appears in. Readers always write in, sometimes with questions for you, or to provide you with a column idea. And, if you're listed in the phone book, be prepared for phone calls from readers. (It's probably a good idea not to be listed, since you may get some crackpots or lonely souls calling you.)

There's a strange aspect to all this columnist business. Freelance columnists who work at home lead a very lonely existence while they're cranking out columns, even if they are on the phone much of the time with sources. Some columnists even become reclusive, buried under stacks of paper, pens, pencils, and publications. If they are housewife-columnists, the laundry piles up, the dirty dishes stack up, and the family eats frozen or canned food a few days a week and eats at a drive-in the rest of the time. This was the case with one of my former students who was a columnist for two years. Sadly, she quit because the job was taking its toll on her family life.

Yet, the flip side is that when you're not being creative at your typewriter or computer, you're out among a lot of people observing and/or gathering information for your next column.

• **Make Your Point in a Way that the Masses Will Understand.** You must work at explaining things simply, no matter how complicated the topic. For example, if you're writing an informational column drawing from your professional expertise, your information must be written simply enough for the layperson to understand. It must also be a topic which can be covered within your limited space. These two things are especially hard for professionals to remember, in that many resort to technical jargon in their field, and they are used to writing communications such as reports which run on for pages. Keep this in mind if you're writing your column for the general public: pretend that you are explaining something to an impatient client who isn't very bright or educated. In a typical consumer publication or general interest publication, remember that your readership may not be very literate. It's especially important for you to write in relatively short sentences so that people can grasp your ideas without rereading long sentences crammed with too many facts.

Even if you're writing for a trade publication, your audience will be refreshed by writing that is succinct, not turgid. After all, professionals have little time to waste.

• **Be Fair and Accurate With Your Facts.** These are the tenets of being a journalist. Be fair by always discussing both sides of an issue—even quoting someone with a different opinion. Further, be accurate with your facts on which you base your opinions and/or advice.

• **Be Expressive and Conversational.** Many people who are articulate verbally, are not expressive on paper. You can learn to be expressive in print if you regularly read famous columnists and pick up their techniques of using anecdotes and examples to illustrate their points.

• **Be Courageous.** Have the courage to say what you really think, instead of what you think people want you to say. Be frank. Write with passion. Don't hold back!

As a columnist, you can't be wishy-washy on a topic. Take a firm stand. Try to write about controversial issues or ones where there is room for disagreement or discussion. At least pick topics which are in real need of public awareness. For example, how do you feel about professional women who are single by choice (not divorced or widowed) who want to have children and raise them alone? Do you think they are selfish? That they aren't really thinking of the child? If so, sound off with your opinions, but also get quotes from women who are doing this and who disagree with you. Incidentally, if you don't know of any women who are doing this, there are organizations and groups of single, professional mothers by choice whom you could contact. For listings of these organizations, consult the *Encyclopedia of Associations* at your public library. (In fact, every columnist should use this book as a resource guide for information on every organization imaginable which would lead you to whatever information you're seeking. Of course, also use this book for its listings of publications produced by organizations which you could write columns for.)

Don't overlook the need to choose a topic which has room for all kinds of discussion. Consider the fact that many columnists fail because they simply write about blah subjects that don't even need to be brought up. Often, in small newspapers, but even in large metropolitan publications, you'll witness a columnist waste valuable space, and eventually you'll see them replaced by another columnist in that very space. If you're simply reporting on a current topic, without giving your opinion, and you're not offering the subject as a means to make a moral point, then it constitutes a news or feature article— not a column. For example, I recently read a column in a local paper where the columnist wrote about how local police officers should be provided with warmer uniforms to wear to help them during the winter months. No room for disagreement or enlightenment there! Why was it written as a column?

- **Have Opinions About Everything!** If you lack opinions, you'll certainly lose your appeal with readers because you won't be entertaining them. They won't perceive you as an interesting individual because you don't have opinions that they can agree or disagree with. In addition to the curse of lacking opinions, there is also a problem if your opinions are predictable. Have you previously covered topics which are all too similar and are you saying virtually the same thing? If so, you'll also lose your audience.

- **Write With Common Sense.** This sounds easier than it is. You may have common sense, but can you write in a common sense way? If you're writing a column to offer a solution to an issue or a problem, make sure you can present your argument in a step-by-step way and that it is sound. If you're not sure your solution would make sense to the public, bounce off your arguments on your acquaintances who aren't familiar with the subject. Then write the column.

- **Attract and Please the Public.** Part of this involves putting forth a distinct personality and writing style which readers easily recognize. Erma Bombeck, who often writes about the plight of the everyday homemaker or parent, appears to attract readership by relating to her readers and making them feel she is one of them—someone with the same problems and concerns in life.

  Say, for example, you are writing an informational column, dispensing your professional expertise, such as in a legal or medical advice column. Although it is written in a serious manner, rather than in Bombeck's lighthearted way, you must still do what she does: identify with the reader. To do this, you should write in a way that laypeople can understand, and do so without talking down to them nor placing yourself above them. Don't use phrases like, "You should know that ..." Even if you are instructing readers about a topic, your column shouldn't sound like a school lesson.

Also avoid pedantic language, professional jargon, and difficult vocabulary which your audience may not know.

Further, don't brag about yourself. Avoid, "When I was pursuing my doctorate in psychology at Yale, a professor told me..." This is unnecessary to state. Simply say, "When I was a graduate student..." In your credit line, at the end of your column, if you want to, you can state you have a Ph.D. from Yale, if you feel you must. In fact, this might be appropriate if you are writing for a trade publication for your audience of peers. However, in a general interest publication, I don't feel it's necessary to state your educational credentials since your readers are most interested in your practical credentials. Remember that in the latter case, your audience is going to assume that you're academically qualified to write about your subject matter, anyway. Use precious column space wisely. Your readers want information about your topic; they don't want your resume. (Incidentally, if your purpose in writing a column is to attract a wider clientele, in your credit line, you should write something like, "David Dittleton is a psychologist in Tuscaloosa, Alabama with the Johnson Clinic." Your main purpose, therefore, in the credit line, is to allow prospective clients to locate you.)

• **Cultivate Communication With Your Readers.** If you don't have time to personally respond to each reader's letter—and you'll be surprised at the number you'll get, particularly in response to columns about controversial issues—answer readers' questions or mention their comments in your future columns. (Caution: don't reveal readers' names unless you've been given their written permission. Just initials are fine.) Answering readers' questions in future columns is an especially good approach if they are common questions and problems which would benefit the general public, or if a comment made by a reader reflects the attitude of many among your readership.

Remember that readers are one of your most valuable resources for ideas. Listen to their comments, and you'll come up with ideas for future column topics.

• **Be Ready to Take Flack.** If you're the type of person who can't take criticism, learn to. Readers will often write in with petty and ill-conceived comments about your views. Some readers are less than polite and even resort to personal attacks, which have nothing to do with the column itself. Stay cool !

Realize that editors don't care whether readers like what you have to say or not, as long as they are reading and responding to your column. Consider that even petty letters and comments against you are actually good for you. Strangely enough, many readers like to read a columnist who will cause them to blow off steam—someone they can react to.

When I used to write a column on community issues, I'd always get a stack of hate mail. Someone even wrote in to tell me, "It's time for you to move on, isn't it?" However, my editor was happy with the column because of its response. (He didn't even agree with my views most of the time.)

• **Keep an Open Mind.** One thing that's interesting about being a columnist is that you may start out your column with a particular opinion in mind, but after you've begun writing, your opinion becomes somewhat modified. Often, when you get ideas on paper, the topic begins to make more sense to you, and you see it more clearly. Or, perhaps you've begun to call people to try out your ideas on them and to get feedback, and, in the process, you've changed your mind. Don't be afraid to change your mind on a topic.

• **Don't Be Afraid to Admit You Made a Mistake.** Don't be so proud that you won't admit you either made a mistake and were off target on an issue, or that you've changed your opinion on a topic discussed in a previous column. Many columnists reverse their stands which they've previously aired, after readers sent letters expressing different viewpoints and enlightened them a bit more on a particular subject. For example, I recently read a local column in which the columnist took up the subject of the variety of self-help groups existing in the community. After discussing some of the more offbeat ones, her stand was that she wondered why there had to be so many of these groups—a self-help group for practically every problem, no matter how insignificant. Her argument was why people don't work at solving their own problems alone. However, after she received a lot of mail in opposition to her views, she wrote another column about what her readers told her, and she changed her viewpoint, somewhat. So, especially if you receive criticism about your views on a topic, question yourself: "Was I too harsh? Was I too quick to judge? Did I miss an important point?" Be honest. Would you write that column differently today, knowing your readers' views?

Be humble, too. My experience as a columnist taught me that my opinions aren't etched in stone or even gravel.

• **Read A Lot.** Read magazines, newspapers, newsletters, alumni publications, trade publications in your area of expertise, books—everything which contains material you're interested in. As a professional writer, I write during the day and read publications at night. You should set aside a specific time, not only to write, but also to catch up on your reading. Being thrifty, I check out a lot of publications at my local library.

Strangely enough, when I began writing, my excuse was that I didn't have time to read. However, through the years, I've found that my writing has improved immensely through reading publications, not only stylewise, but in locating ideas to write about. Now, I love reading. In fact, I love reading columnists, especially the ones I feel are particularly good like Ellen Goodman, Mike Royko, and Roger Simon, and I always keep my eyes open for new anthologies of columnists' work. Develop your own list of favorite columnists and read them regularly. Start by exploring the columnists I've described in the appendix of this book and selected anthologies of their work. Then, branch out by reading other anthologies of your choosing by these and other columnists.

As a writer, I accumulate any and all printed matter, and I feel you should, too. The next time you get a newsletter or even an advertisement about something in the mail, do not toss it out until you've inspected it. It may signal a theme or a basic idea which you can incorporate into your next column.

I always pick up free newspapers around town. At some public libraries, there are free magazines through the magazine exchange rack. Current and old magazines are often circulated, so pick these up, too. Don't forget to look in the lobby of the library which often contains stacks of free newspapers and newsletters left by special interest groups. In addition, go to used bookstores and pick up past issues of magazines (but recent ones) for as little as 25 cents. (I have no shame. I've even been known to steal magazines out of the doctor's office if they contain articles which are vital to me.)

At the library, read reference books such as *Writer's Market* which tell you which publications in your subject area of interest will send you free samples. You'll not only get ideas for columns from reading a lot of publications, but you'll also get ideas on what publications might be interested in running your column. It doesn't matter if a publication doesn't currently run columns. If you approach the editor with the idea of running a column, you may be able to sell him on the idea of running yours. Remember, the key words are "sell someone on something." Be like a salesperson! Take the initiative to sell yourself and your column. It's not beneath your dignity as a writer to be a salesperson. It's a necessity.

If you're writing a column about daily living, read lifestyle magazines which run articles about trends and life in the U.S. which you can comment on. In addition, read local newspapers for club and meeting notices, and press releases about events which you can observe or participate in and write about. From these notices, you'll also learn about special interest groups and services which may be the topic of future columns. You can attend these group meetings and write about why people are interested in joining these groups.

When you read newspapers, also look at the classified ads. You can get ideas about businesses, services offered to the public, and trends in this country, such as weight loss clinics. You'll also be able to determine societal values from these.

Familiarize yourself with reference books such as the *Encyclopedia of Associations* (previously referred to). This is a multi-volume book, updated annually, which contains thousands of entries for associations, societies, fraternal clubs, and even fan clubs and radical groups, all categorized by area of interest. There's an association or club for everything these days, from the serious to the lighthearted. As I previously said, you may need to contact an association for information about some type of subject you're writing about. This book will fascinate you. Through the years, this "encyclopedia" has included such entries as, The International Lucille Ball Fan Club, Ladies Against Women, International Organization of Nerds, and Liars Club. (Incidentally, if you were to buy this reference work, it would be very expensive. I found my multi-volume edition, just a few years old, at a thrift shop for only $6. When I run across an entry I'm interested in, I phone the reference hotline at my local library to verify the organization's current address. I feel any serious writer should haunt thrift shops for reference and other books, from just a pocket dictionary to Mike Royko's *Like I Was Sayin.'* I found the latter book there, too.) Also, for your private library, those book sales sponsored by Friends of the Library of your local public library are a must. I should report that my personal library contains thousands of dollars worth of books which I paid 50 cents apiece for at thrift shops and library sales.

As far as "lighter" reading, read the Yellow Pages of the phone book for names of organizations. You can call organizations to have them send you brochures about their services. If their services appeal to you, you can interview people connected with the organizations and write about them in your column.

If you're writing an informational column pertaining to your professional field or about your hobby, read trade journals and association/club newsletters to familiarize yourself with all current issues and advancements in the field which you can comment on in your column. It's amazing how as professionals in a certain field, we sometimes get so wrapped up in the practice of our field (with clients) that we sometimes aren't as religious about keeping up with current trends. Even though you may be a member of your local trade/professional association, you may not be attending its meetings as often as you should. Do so. You'll be amazed at the ideas that come out of these meetings which you can build your columns around.

Informational columns often require researching a topic, especially if you are dealing with an issue which has recently been the subject of many news articles. Read a lot. You may also need to get quotes from pertinent people involved with this issue, and sometimes you need go no further than to call upon your local colleagues whom you've met at association meetings.

Choosing Your Type Of Column/Becoming Successful

In choosing the type of column you want to write, you can consider a number of factors. Of course, you should consider your interests, experiences, background, hobbies, and profession. However, you should also ask yourself: "What is motivating me to become a columnist?" (1) Do I simply like to write? (2) Do I want a supplemental source of income while I stay at home? (3) Do I want prestige from the general public? (4) Do I want to draw more clients into my business? (5) Do I want my peers in my field to respect me?

If you said "yes" to the last two questions, you obviously want to write a column drawing upon your professional expertise. You may be the kind of person who is most proud—

out of all your accomplishments—of your professional achievements. However, will you enjoy the actual writing of the column or will it be drudgery? And, does your professional life give you so much joy, enough joy, so that you will love to spend additional time focusing upon it while writing your column? Or, would you rather spend your time away from your office totally removed from your profession, doing some leisure activity? Be honest with yourself. Writing this type of column may burn you out and even cause you to burn out at your actual business practice.

Consider, too, that if your informational column really took off and you became syndicated or even just a sought-after consultant, if you would be willing to leave your business practice to become a full-time writer and celebrity traveling to give speaking engagements. No, I'm not joking. It can happen. It's possible that an activity such as column writing which began solely as a means of attracting clientele and building up your business practice, ironically negates the need for your business in its present form. Needless to say, these are things you must consider.

As an alternative, in writing a column, you may want to escape from your professional life by writing about one of your hobbies. For example, I knew a psychiatrist who, in his spare time, became a local movie critic, writing a weekly column.

Just as important as these considerations, what type of column do you see as being the most marketable, given the way our society is progressing? And, what kind of column would offer the public something in the way of information that it usually doesn't get from other columnists?

Let's go back to the beginning of this section, when I asked you to consider what was motivating you to become a columnist. If you're a homemaker or retiree, for example, and you simply like to write and want a supplemental source of income while you stay at home, you'll find that being a columnist is both personally rewarding and affords you the recognition and prestige that stay-at-home people don't always get these days. After all, we're living in a society where the go-getter out in the job world is the one whose life is acknowledged and validated by others. Now, stay-at-homers, it's time to stand up and be counted!

Are you prepared for success? Whoever you are, home-maker, retiree, professional, or hobbyist, you can be a successful writer and columnist. The world of journalism is a strange and whimsical one. Many famous journalists, in fact, never studied journalism in school, and a lot of them never went to college. Columnist Mike Royko, for one, didn't. In fact, he has criticized people who are very educated for being too educated and not practical enough—his son, the Ph.D., namely.

Although I'm biased because of my non-journalistic academic background—I studied and received degrees in foreign languages—there is no need to study journalism in school. Journalistic writing skills can easily be picked up, and of course, the objective of this book is to teach you this. (Besides, journalism schools don't necessarily turn out good writers, because the course of study often focuses on theory, history and law of the press, and ethics, rather than the practical craft of writing.)

Liberal arts backgrounds are very useful to journalists, so if you have one, you're lucky. Syndicated columnist Ellen Goodman, for example, entered the world of journalism after a liberal arts background at Radcliffe College. The most important attribute for a journalistic writer to have is to be willing to cultivate a broad background and a stimulated mind with a thirst to keep learning and informing oneself. The liberal arts foster this.

As I mentioned previously, a lot of columnists who are syndicated are on the staffs of major publications, and their work became syndicated from the exposure they were getting from writing for those publications. Syndicates then approached them. However, syndicated columnist Erma Bombeck didn't get her start from being a staff writer. In fact, her example is a good one which you should follow and benefit from. Bombeck started writing a column for a small weekly newspaper on a freelance basis. In fact, she practically gave her column away for nothing. The exposure, however, served her well. After writing for the weekly paper, a daily paper in the region noticed her column and wanted it, offering her more money. With the daily newspaper which had a much larger circulation, she received even more exposure. Then, along came a syndicate which saw her work and offered her syndication and national exposure. The moral of this, is start small and work your way up, just as the college graduate who goes out in the job world and works his way up the ladder, little by little.

As we'll be discussing in detail later, your goal, in the beginning, should be just to get into print, even if it means starting as a columnist at a weekly newspaper, small professional newsletter, or small trade magazine. Later, the big-time metropolitan daily newspapers and prestigious magazines come along. (Unless, of course, you have high contacts at the latter, now.)

In writing for a general interest publication, you should try to get your material published locally, then move on to a regional market, and finally a national one. Build exposure little by little. You may even be able to bypass the regional market, if you're lucky. When you've gotten significant exposure, approach prestigious publications or a syndicate. Reaching the big-time works like a charm, if you go step-by-step.

What comes after syndication? As a syndicated columnist, you can become an author, just by collecting your published columns in an anthology. You may even become a best-selling author.

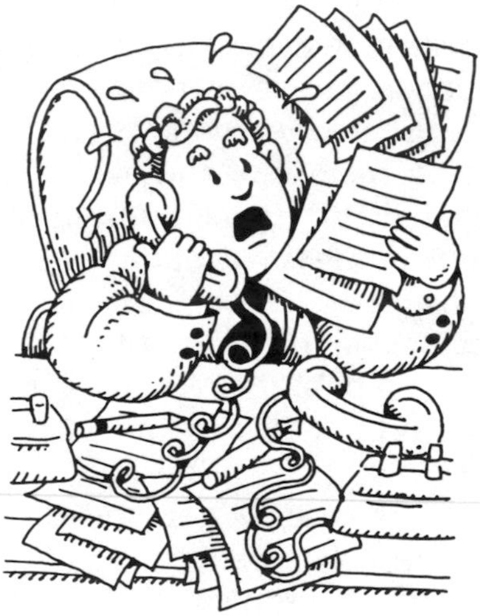

Chapter 2

COLUMN WRITING BASICS

You must reorient your thinking if you are going to write columns. There is no room in column writing, nor in journalistic writing in general, for the English composition style which you learned throughout your school days. It simply won't work, and editors won't take the time to re-write your piece.

In any journalistic piece, and column writing is no exception, you must begin with a snappy sentence to grab the reader's attention and draw him into your topic. Then, you must build your argument, stating it in a very explicit way, using specific examples, leaving no facts to the reader's imagination. That is, your information and opinions should be cut-and-dried, and you shouldn't wait until the end of your column to state or work up to your most important points. You must give different examples to illustrate your thesis, and let them be just that—not the same example repeated nor restated in just a slightly different way.

Beginning journalistic writers have a terrible time with redundancy because they think back to their English composition school days when they were told to state their basic point in the beginning, reiterate it in the middle, and again at the end. You were supposed to build up to the climax, too.

As a columnist, particularly if you're writing a creative column about life and living, you may, of course, want to build your column around an anecdote, and in the end, finally make your point. This is fine, and this is one instance in which you wouldn't go clippity-clip in stating your points and building your arguments. However, even in taking the anecdotal route, you still must at least give the reader the notion that you will soon get to your point, and you must be spending your time entertaining him along the way until you get to it. Otherwise, the reader will merely get bored, and wonder if you are taking him anywhere, and he may set your column down on the table never bothering to finish reading it.

In column writing, you really can't take the time to drag your reader through paragraph after paragraph of relatively innocuous facts and background, and save the important stuff until later. Some syndicated columnists like Mike Royko often take the roundabout route before making their basic points, but you will notice they are highly-skilled writers who are so entertaining that they take you along an interesting route, sustaining your interest all along. If you are not a very skilled writer, I would not recommend using a very long anecdote, unless you are certain that you have such an interesting story to tell that you can maintain the readers' interest. You're safe with a short anecdote, but if you want to go with a long one, test it out on a friend or relative first, before offering it to the public.

In writing a column, above all, remember that you are not writing a novel where your reader can interpret things among a variety of possibilities. A reader must clearly be able to understand exactly what points you are making. It's not unusual for novice writers to begin writing and later realize that they aren't even sure of their points. It goes without saying that you can't convince your audience of what you're trying to say, if you're not clear about them yourself.

Although all of this may sound obvious to you, in the course of this book, we'll be looking very closely at a variety of columns, and you'll soon see that it's so easy for a beginning writer to fall into the non-journalistic way of writing, or even just to produce bad writing, in general.

Before we turn to the first column, which is an example of a bad one, we need to look at some details and examples of typical journalistic writing. We'll touch on them now, briefly, and take them up in detail in subsequent chapters.

First, let's touch on the lead sentence (your first sentence) and your lead paragraph. In your first sentence, you want to start out with a bang or at least some statement to lure the reader on. Sometimes columnists use a play on words (a pun) or a cliché which they can substantiate or disprove. Or, sometimes they use a simile, metaphor, or some other descriptive device to grab the reader's attention.

As an alternative, sometimes the lead sentence hints at what the column is about and hooks the reader so he'll discover the topic.

Let's take a look at examples of each of the above.

(1) **Play on Words.** Suppose you are writing an informational column about how to easily obtain credit. You may want to start out with a hypothetical example of someone (or even a real example if you receive the person's written permission) who has been successful at getting credit.

> Example: You've got to give Tom Mason credit. Everyone else does. In fact, he's got 42 credit cards.

As another example of a play on words, let's look at this hypothetical lead sentence to a column on a community issue.

> Example: John Jones, city traffic engineer, is telling residents on the southwest side, where to get off, and this has raised quite a furor.

(If you use a lead sentence of this kind, in the following sentence, you would allow the reader to discover the meaning behind this lead sentence, by stating: "Exit 50 ramp of Western Freeway is off limits to them, and they must drive five miles out of their way to get off at Exit 54. ")

(2) **A Cliché to Substantiate, Disprove, or Take Off On.** Suppose you are writing an informational column about the need to invest in stocks before the stock market soars, you may want to use a lead sentence like: "As the saying goes, 'it's better late than never,' but now is just the right time to invest in stocks. "

As for starting out with another cliché, look at this lead sentence concerning a column about a magician: "The hand is quicker that the eye, as you've heard magicians say, but magician Tom White believes that the key to being good at the job also involves the ability to entertain."

Incidentally, I wouldn't advice you to use more than one cliché in your column, otherwise the reader will get caught up in clichés.

There is also another common method of using a cliché, by taking off on a familiar one. Consider this hypothetical lead sentence which a music critic could use in his column: "When they were passing out the class, Dionne Warwick was first in line." Obviously, this takes off on the cliché, "When they were passing out the brains, (so and so) was first in line."

You can also take a twist on a familiar cliché. Consider this hypothetical lead sentence which a food columnist could use: "What's becoming more American than apple pie? Pizza. "

(3) **Simile/Metaphor.** A simile creates a comparison between two things through use of the word "like" or "as." For example, if you're writing an informational column about how small business people should in-

crease their business by not just offering their mail order customers a toll-free number to place their order, but credit besides, you could use this simile in your lead sentence to grab the reader's attention: "Offering your mail order customers a toll-free number to place their order, but not extending them credit card use, is like offering a restaurant patron steak without a knife."

Also, consider a lead sentence which contains a metaphor, that is, when two different things with seemingly no relation to each other are linked, thereby resulting in a literally impossible claim. Let's take a hypothetical column about a woman working in a predominately male field, and let's form this lead sentence: "Jane Smith is a splash of perfume in her workplace." (The metaphor is "Jane Smith" and "splash of perfume.")

(4) **Hinting at the Column's Topic.** This hypothetical lead sentence could introduce a column about the problems of disabled people: "They sit at their window for hours, catching glimpses of activity in surrounding high-rise units." (Obviously, here the reader wants to read on to find out who "they" are. In a column of this kind, after this lead sentence, you could even focus on just one disabled person to illustrate the common problems of the disabled.)

In general, in writing lead sentences, avoid beginning your column with trite phrases. For example, if you are writing a column on community happenings and are covering an annual event, do not write the following: "Well, it's that time of year again."

Another inappropriate lead sentence is, "Years ago, in the old days..." If you do the latter, for example, the reader's reaction will be, "Oh, no, this old duffer-columnist is going to reminisce. Must be boring, so I'll turn the page."

It's sometimes okay to begin an informational column with a lead sentence which is a question. However, make it an interesting one which will urge the reader onward. For example, if you are an attorney who is writing a legal advice column on the importance of making out a will, your lead sentence should not be, "Have you made out a will?" Instead, draw the reader into your column with this dramatic lead sentence: "Dying without a will could result in heartache for your heirs."

As for column structure, keep your paragraphs short with two or three sentences. Even a one-sentence paragraph is fine if it's important information which you want to stand out. Short paragraphs are typical of journalistic writing, particularly in newspapers. Exceptions to short paragraphs are found in some of the more formal publications like the *Wall Street Journal* and *The New York Times*, besides some magazines. The journalistic idea behind short paragraphs is that they are more readable to the eye, so readers of general interest publications who are in a hurry and often scan pieces quickly, can easily do so.

As for content, be as thorough as possible with your information and opinions. After you've written a column, there should be no question in readers' minds about the topic you've written about, the facts behind it, and the opinions you have. Do not assume, for example, that your reader is already familiar with the major sides of the issue you're writing about, simply because the issue has been aired a lot in the news. Assume that this is the first time the reader has heard about the issue. Your column should touch the major points of the issue which have already been in the news, along with new points and opinions you are bringing to light.

As I said previously and will continue to stress, do not assume your reader knows the answer to something. Spell out all possible facts to questions the reader may have. Leave no facts to the imagination of the reader. If you're writing for a general interest type of publication, assume your reader is ignorant of the particular issue. (However, if you are writing for your peers in a trade publication, you may assume a certain level of knowledge on the part of your audience.)

In your content, you shouldn't forget details. Say you

write a column about a lottery winner and how his winnings have changed his life. If you quote him as saying, "It's a great feeling knowing I can afford to buy anything," ask him what some of the most expensive possessions he's bought are, and how much he's paid for them.

As another example of including all details, if you are writing a column about your favorite sport of kayaking, you must give your reader enough information about the sport and excite him so that he'll want to try it. For example, how fast can one go in a kayak? How is kayaking different from other kinds of canoeing? Also touch on practical facts and details, such as what some of the more interesting maneuvers are which one can do in a kayak and specifically what they entail. Further, how does one paddle? Do your legs or knees get tired, and how can you curtail this tired feeling? You can even cover details such as how much it costs to rent a kayak. Remember that besides your facts, your piece should contain subjectivity, such as why you love the sport. Subjectivity is what makes your piece a column.

Along these same lines of content, do not make factual statements which contain holes in content. Figure out what's wrong with this example: "Between 1860 to 1914, many Polish immigrants arrived in America." How many is "many Polish immigrants?" This sentence sounds like a report written by a grade schooler!

We can make another point about the content of factual statements. Do not, for example, make references to historical events unless you mention exactly when they occurred. For example, don't mention that the California Gold Rush attracted Polish immigrants, unless you state when the Gold Rush occurred. Avoid making your readers do encyclopedic research when you can easily provide them with a date.

I once read a column where the lead sentence contained factual loopholes which were never clarified in the rest of the column. The lead sentence was: "Irish-American immigrants came to the U.S. in three primary surges, and today they are one of the largest ethnic groups in the country." After reading this lead sentence, I expected the next sentence to clarify the years of the surges and give the number of Irish immigrants in the U.S. today. As I said, journalists should get right to the point with specifics. However, in this case, not only did the second sentence fail to reveal this information, but nowhere in the column were these points clarified. Amazing!

Further, never make your reader have to wait to receive basic information until late in the column, when you can give him the information in summarized form in the early stages, and then develop these facts in detail later, if necessary. Do not, I stress, use the English composition style of being vague with details until you reveal them at the very end.

As far as content, I've also read columns which began with historical trivia which wasn't interesting and therefore made the column sound like a high school textbook. For example, if you are an attorney writing an informational column about the importance of having a will, you don't need to mention (as I once read in a column) that the first will was written in Egypt in 2548 B.C. After all, this is not relevant to why the reader should make out his will. Always keep in mind that the reader will wonder about insignificant or irrelevant facts, and he'll ask himself, "Why am I being told this?"

Further along the lines of content, define terms that need defining and explain them in laypeople's language. And, do not wait until the end of your column to finally define what they mean. I've seen many columnists refer to a relatively obscure term a few times throughout their column, and literally keep the reader in suspense about its meaning until the end.

For example, if you're a doctor, don't assume that everyone knows what multiple sclerosis is. Remember that people hear so many terms, that they often confuse one with another if the terms have similar sounding names. If there's any doubt in your mind that someone doesn't know the meaning of a term, define it. What, specifically, is autism? Define it.

In addition, don't make references to Parkinson's Law or Murphy's Law without explaining what they mean. And, say you're writing about a complex topic such as reincarnation, what does it mean in its entirety? What does it involve in all of its aspects? Clarify the term. Do people have any misconceptions about it? If so, discuss them.

In general, if a column topic is too complex, too technical, or just too long to describe in the column's space, then you obviously must choose another topic to write about.

Among other content offenses, do not forget to tell your readers what an acronym stands for. On first reference, you can use the name in full. On following references, use the acronym only. For example, if there was a group called Frustrated Housewives United, its acronym would be FHU.

Direct quotes are a major element in most columns, but they often are used in a meaningless way, and therefore they adversely affect the column's general content. First of all, if you quote someone make sure the quote is understandable. This is obvious, you say? Well, I can't even count the number of times I've read direct quotes in journalistic pieces which make absolutely no sense at all. Not only beginning writers fall into this trap, but even experienced journalists sometimes do. Some writers will interview a person and in the context of the interview, the quote seems to make sense. However, the quote becomes confusing in print before a reader who was not present when it was said and didn't have the benefit of hearing the whole conversation.

Make sure that your direct quotes aren't vague or contradictory. Often, beginning writers have trouble judging whether a quote really is specific enough. For example, in a student's paper I read, a former drug addict was quoted as saying, "I really don't know why I began using drugs. Nothing in my life was missing ... I don't think drug slavery is necessarily physical, but spiritual. By spiritual, I mean a craving within. Something not quite complete in a soul that desperately reaches out and tries to right itself." In this quote, the first two sentences are vague. After all, something must have been missing in the drug addict's life—as most of us would agree—if he turned to drugs. What follows these two sentences, contradicts them. Besides, that talk about the soul is so vague, that it is nothing but rhetoric.

Obviously, if you interview a person who is giving you vague statements or answers such as the above, be prepared to ask for a clarification of what he means. Ask: "Do you mean to say that ..." Try to get him to rephrase his statement in comprehensible terms. Two words which journalists always use to force people to clarify their statements are "how" or "why." These words will usually get poor or evasive communicators to straighten up. However, if the person is such a poor communicator that you can't get him to say anything quotable, try interviewing someone else.

If the direct quote is not completely clear, but you feel you can easily get it clarified, try to get the interviewee to reword it. Do not fill in missing words when quoting someone, unless they are essential to clarify the meaning. If they are essential, then put those missing words in parentheses so that the reader will surmise that the writer inserted them.

> Example: "We've been trying to come up with a cure for years," Dr. Jones said.

> Rewritten: "We've been trying to come up with a cure (for cancer) for years," Dr. Jones said.

In an informational column, especially when quoting people of authority, be extra careful not to fill in words haphazardly nor alter their quotes in some major way. In this case, it would be very easy to inadvertently alter the meaning or change the nuance of what they said. Be sure not to alter quotes giving vital information which can be misconstrued, such as those from doctors or lawyers. If their quotes are vague, ask them for a clarification in "laypeople's language."

In the case of interviewing a person who uses slang, but

who says something quotable, don't quote him in a cleaned-up version. Go with the slang. Column writing is supposed to be conversational, and of course, slang lends to the conversational effect. Do not use the slang, however, if you feel the interviewee didn't mean to use it, or that he slipped up with bad grammar. In short, don't embarrass your interviewee.

It's interesting to note, when reading the work of many professional journalists, that they generally prefer to follow their quotes with "he said," rather than saying "he remarked," "he commented," "he noted," and other substitutions. Many feel that the "he said" does not get monotonous, but that instead, it blends into the dialogue, quote after quote.

Also, when you quote someone, do not say, "He said the following," and then proceed to quote him. In journalistic style, it's better to quote the person and then follow the quote with "he said."

> Example: John Smith and his supporters are irate about the proposed tax hike and recently took to the streets to protest it. "It's clearly unfair," Smith said. "We plan to gather 20,000 signatures during the next five weeks."

> (Also note, that the "Smith said" breaks up the quote so that you don't lose the reader by stating two consecutive sentences, before you identify who is talking.)

Realize, that journalists often like to isolate a quote in a single paragraph to make it more readable.

> Example:
> "We've been trying to come up with a cure (for cancer) for years," Dr. Jones said.

> Jones, who has been on the staff of Mercy Hospital for 30 years, is optimistic that a cure will be found in this decade.

I stress again that you should not lose control of your column with excessive direct quotes, particularly a string of successive ones, unless you're recreating a conversation that took place. (Successive direct quotes used to recreate dialogue—for the effect of immediacy and realism—are certainly appropriate in a creative type of column.) However, try to avoid a succession of direct quotes in an informational column without breaking here and there with narration.

If you are recounting a conversation in a creative column, be selective in what you choose as the dialogue. Don't bore your reader with every single sentence that was said, unless it is absolutely relevant.

As columnists, Mike Royko and Erma Bombeck are great examples of ones who often use a lot of direct quotes for recreating an actual conversation or even fabricating one for humorous purposes. They are highly skilled at this technique, and do not include extraneous statements, so read their columns regularly if you want to pick up this skill, too.

As another point on direct quotes, from now on, when you read a journalistic piece, realize that journalists often use a direct quote early in their piece to grab the reader's attention and draw him into the piece. Keep this in mind when you write.

In general, you should use direct quotes:

- to recreate a conversation
- when someone says something in an interesting or colorful way which, for example, reveals a facet of his personality
- when someone gives an opinion which would lose something if you paraphrased it
- if someone said something really important which you wanted your reader to pay particular attention to
- if someone provided you with authoritative information which you needed to attribute to him because he was the expert

Remember never to quote someone if he said something which you could easily put into your own words.

A Few More Words

Many of the points I've discussed so far in this chapter sound pretty basic, and in a lot of cases, downright obvious. However, I challenge any beginning writer to be able to carry out these points without making mistakes. They are hard to implement when you actually try them. Yes, it's hard to remember to keep your most interesting points or your most important information high (early) in your piece if it's an informational column. It's hard to break that old school habit of burying your important points until late in the piece. (Just the other day I wrote a piece—a business letter—and I found I wrote it "in reverse." That is, I made some of my important points at the end. So, if I can write in reverse, you can bet that a beginning writer often ends up with a final sentence which should have been his lead sentence.)

Further, as a writer, beginning or professional, it's hard to grab the reader's attention with an interesting lead sentence and hold his attention. Sometimes, I still take 15 minutes or more just to come up with a good lead sentence.

Remember, too, that you shouldn't cram too much information into any one paragraph. In addition, the sequence of your paragraphs must be clear and logical. To do so, you need smooth transitions between each one—the last sentence of one paragraph and the first sentence of the next one should lead into each other logically.

If you go on to a new subject, rather than just start a new paragraph, you must signal to your reader that you're going on to something new by using transitional words such as "aside from this," "on the other hand," or "in addition to this." Whatever you do, instead of using a transitional word or phrase, don't say something like, "Changing the subject, now I will deal with..." I've seen this done in published columns.

In addition, be logical at all times. Do not discuss a point, then leave it, pick up a new point, and later, return to discussing your previous point. Keep your arguments logical for readers to follow. As a bad example, I once read a column about the writer's frustration with moving from one house to another, year after year. This columnist really confused me with his lack of logical sequence. He talked about the hassle of packing, the hassle of trucking his belongings to a new home, unpacking at the new place, and then he'd flip-flop from one of these topics to the other. What a mess and an unnecessary one at that!

Given the basics of column writing which you are now familiar with, read the following fabricated column. Some basic themes are taken from my students' papers, but largely the column is fabricated (as are other columns in this book) to illustrate elements we've discussed. As you will find, this column has several errors which you should avoid when constructing your own columns. All names and facts in the column are fictitious.

After reading the column, test yourself and jot down your own comments about its flaws. Before you read the column's subsequent commentary, number the column's paragraphs so you can readily follow my comments.

Note: never fabricate informational columns. I've done so only as an instructional tool.

This is the column:

Times have changed since the good old days when I was of childbearing age. Now, we see the childbirth trend which allows fathers in the delivery room. Many people don't think this is a wonderful innovation in our modern society. In fact, there are many who believe that a lot of men aren't fit to view this most dramatic scene, and that even worse, they turn out to be disruptive to the delivery process.

Joan Cavanaugh, a recently retired Irish nurse in Providence, and Jayne Seymour, a retired nurse in Baltimore oppose husbands being allowed in the delivery room. They have had solid, rewarding, and interesting careers as delivery room nurses. Cavanaugh graduated from Cornell University School of Nursing in

1945, and worked for 40 years as a nurse, including service in the Viet Nam War. Seymour graduated from Cornell in 1946 and worked for 39 years as a nurse.

During her career, Cavanaugh was the only nurse in Rhode Island to have received three "Nurse of the Year" awards for her excellence and dedication: in 1963, 1975, and 1981. Seymour received a "Nurse of the Year" award in Maryland in 1953.

Cavanaugh is a mother and grandmother. She married at 39, and had a son at 40 (now an electrical engineer). At 41, she had twin daughters, one of whom is now a teacher, the other, now a surgical nurse in New York City. She was widowed at 44 and raised small children while working long, exhausting shifts. In modern day terms, Cavanaugh would be called "Supermom." Seymour has never been married.

Cavanaugh proudly claims to have aided in the delivery of 6,513 babies during her career. "I simply loved it," she said. "I still keep a personal log of each birth with each baby's name. The log is 300 pages long —a book! To think, I almost went into geriatric care nursing. I'm glad I didn't. Helping to deliver each baby for me was still as exciting in my older years as when I first got started in the Dark Ages," Cavanaugh said with a chuckle. Cavanaugh added that the Dark Ages was when "the father's welcome mat didn't grace the delivery room's door."

To summarize why Cavanaugh is qualified to address this topic, the vital points to recognize are that she helped to deliver babies for about four decades—in the old and new eras of child birthing; she is a mother herself, having been through the birthing experience; and she has gained the recognition from her peers as being a nurse who was totally dedicated to her work.

Seymour is another medical professional who simply doesn't favor fathers in the delivery room, and she said that in her later years of nursing, she longed for the old times when they weren't admitted.

On the opposing side, proponents of fathers in the delivery room feel that they have a God-given right to participate in this memorable event. They believe that their being on hand is an asset throughout the mother's emotional ordeal, since they calm their wives who are often fearful and anxious. Further, they feel their presence allows male bonding with the newborn at this crucial time.

While many fathers may help in the process, others do not, according to Cavanaugh and Seymour, who feel that they can get in the way. Often, fathers urge the process on too quickly, upsetting the natural scheme, and the delivery becomes even more trying for the mother, they explained.

Seymour added: "It's simply not always a great idea for women to have husbands as coaches because all too often fathers are overwhelmed by all the natural details they are witnessing." She further explained: "Some fathers turn really pale. They can't handle all the gory aspects they are confronted with. All the blood gushing out, for instance, that we medical professionals are used to. It's not a pretty scene, to say the least, and it makes some dads sick to their stomachs. Some even start feeling light-headed and faint."

Cavanaugh said that men who suffer these adverse effects during the experience are too embarrassed to excuse themselves from the room, fearing that they'll be regarded as not being strong and brave enough—"wimps even." She said, too, that the nurse is burdened with having to worry about the father, besides. Worse, the mothers sense their husbands' discomfort and this adds to the women's anxiety. Cavanaugh said there are other problems, too, and that mothers should always be considered first in this situation.

As Seymour sees it, some fathers she's known don't really want to witness the birth, but they believe they should because now it's the accepted custom, unlike in their fathers' era. They also think they'll be frowned upon or laughed at by their male friends if they don't participate, and that more importantly, their wives will be disappointed with them.

Though many will concur with the good nurses, many nurses, doctors, and parents will certainly take issue with their comments. But considering Cavanaugh's qualifications in the field and those of Seymour, and their frank assessment, this topic should be reexamined by women of childbearing age, their husbands, and even by the medical profession.

My opinion is that there's a great deal to be said for the good old-fashioned way of birthing with the private sign engraved on the delivery room door, and the men sitting in the waiting room—where they belong!

Commentary

In general, this column has major problems with redundancy, trite expressions, and of course, content and structure. This column offers merely a one-sided point of view without giving different examples of people who disagree with Cavanaugh and Seymour. A good columnist adequately brings both sides of the issue to light. For example, what about the viewpoint of a midwife? The writer never even bothers to give her own opinion until the very end—she merely relies on the nurses to give hers. We never even find out why this writer chose to deal with the topic. We wonder: what was her own experience with childbirth? Early on in the column, the writer takes up too much space giving the two nurses' biographical information and details which are irrelevant and boring, rather than getting to the heart of the topic—a breach of journalistic style. The writer gradually works up to the issue, as is done in the English composition style, that which you are to avoid.

Paragraph 1. The lead sentence is trite with "the good old days." From this lead sentence, I would expect the writer to be introducing a column in which she speaks of her own experience. However, it soon becomes evident, that she will be discussing the views of others.

Paragraphs 2 & 3. Instead of giving the reader the biographies of Cavanaugh and Seymour, the writer could have woven in biographical facts about them, here and there, throughout the column. In paragraph 3, the writer, however, did do something right. She refers to Cavanaugh and Seymour by their last names. It is common journalistic style to refer to a person on second and following references by his/her last name, without using courtesy titles such as "Ms." or "Mr." This is pointed out in *The Associated Press Stylebook and Libel Manual* (and other style manuals) which many journalists follow. Some publications deviate from this style, though I would recommend your using it as a general practice, unless the publication you write for gives you other instructions.

Paragraph 4. More unessential biographical information, except for the fact that we're told Cavanaugh is a mother and grandmother. The fact that her son is an electrical engineer in New York City is irrelevant. The fact that one of her daughters is a nurse could be relevant, and we later wonder why Cavanaugh fails to mention whether her nurse-daughter shares her perspective on this topic. As for her other daughter, maybe this teacher-daughter has children and Cavanaugh could also have mentioned what her perspective is on fathers in the delivery room.

Paragraph 5. This paragraph should have come earlier. This information could have been included, for example, in the third paragraph.

Paragraph 6. This reads like an English composition. It's unnecessary to summarize the vital points because we already know Cavanaugh worked for four decades in the old and new birthing eras, that she's a mother, and that she was a dedicated nurse.

Paragraph 7. This paragraph is redundant. We found out in paragraph 2 about this.

Paragraph 8. This paragraph could have been integrated into the first paragraph.

Paragraph 9. This paragraph should have come in the beginning when Cavanaugh and Seymour were introduced. (After the first sentence of paragraph 2).

Paragraph 10. Here again, this paragraph should have come early on. Journalists always attempt to use a quote early in their piece to grab the reader's attention and draw him into the piece, and this quote could have been the one.

Paragraph 11. Whether you agree with Cavanaugh or not, one wonders how common the problems are with fathers in the delivery room. The writer should have asked Cavanaugh if she feels it's a problem most of the time or just some of the time, and whether a father has ever confided his difficulty to her. The writer could have gotten a quote from a man who's benefited from the experience and one who found it hard to take. (The latter quote could have been used anonymously, if embarrassment to the father was a concern.) Also, the writer could have gotten a quote from an anonymous mother who felt the experience had been too trying for her husband, and another mother who felt her husband aided her by being on hand during the delivery. And, we wonder, what about Cavanaugh's son? Is he a father who could be quoted? What about her sons-in-law? Further, in the last sentence of this paragraph, it is useless to say, "There are other problems, too" without identifying just what they are. (Journalists always try to avoid such unspecific statements, and others like, "there are many other reasons." Also avoid usage of "etc.")

Paragraph 12. Here again, an anonymous quote from a father who felt this way should have been included.

Paragraph 13. As in the first sentence, always avoid trite expressions like "the good nurses." Further, this whole first sentence is obvious and doesn't even need to be said. I would have liked to see a quote from a nurse with an opposing viewpoint. In the second sentence, it's okay, as the writer has done, to start the sentence with the word "but. " Journalists often start sentences with words like "and," "but," and "instead," (as I've done throughout this book), even though I remember my high school English teacher used to say these were no-nos. One last point: a reader would be interested in finding out from Cavanaugh and Seymour whether they feel a lot of medical professionals or just some medical professionals agree with them.

Paragraph 14. As I mentioned previously, the writer doesn't get to her own opinion until the very end. Her opinion based on her own experience is a relevant part of the column. It's simply not sufficient to imply where you stand and let others do the talking for you, such as in this case, where Cavanaugh and Seymour are giving opinions throughout, on the columnist's behalf, it seems. Just how does this columnist feel? She could have personalized the column with either her own experience or that of her relatives. Does this columnist have a daughter, a niece, or even a granddaughter of childbearing age who has recently given birth? If not, does she personally know of young women who've had a bad experience with modern birthing? What examples can the columnist herself give?

On the other hand, if this columnist has absolutely no connection with the childbirth experience, why did she write a column on such a topic? Columnists usually take on topics which they have some personal connection or interest in. We wonder, then, was this column written merely to give publicity to the nurses—friends of hers, perhaps? This column reads merely like a straightforward interview with the nurses to air their views. It could, therefore, have been just a regular feature article on the nurses, rather than have taken up column space.

The columnist's conclusion isn't even realistic. Is she saying that no fathers should be allowed in the delivery room? After all, if some fathers aren't prepared to be in the delivery room and view the experience, maybe health professionals could better train fathers, in general, by offering better instruction and classes in childbirth ahead of time. Perhaps the health professions need to make more resources available to fathers before the birth experience through public awareness campaigns, for example.

As for other points in this last paragraph, avoid saying "my opinion is that," or "I feel that," since the reader already knows you're stating an opinion. Too, avoid the trite expression, "the good old-fashioned..."

Final Words

Before you submit a column to an editor, have someone who is a perceptive person read it to ensure that the information is clear and explained thoroughly, that your arguments are logically presented, that you have smooth transitions between paragraphs, and that your direct quotes make sense.

Often, ideas which make sense to the writer who is too close to his subject and his writing, are vague to others. This is especially true of confusing direct quotes. Remember, if you interviewed someone and he said something in the context of the interview, it may make sense to you, but not to the reader who wasn't present during the interview.

And, if you quote someone, make sure the quote is accurate. Repeat the quote to him, after he has said it, if it's controversial subject matter. Sometimes people are quick to say things that they later regret they said, so it's also a good idea to keep notes of your conversation with them.

Do not, however, let the interviewee read your column before it goes into print. It's not the interviewee's business to approve of your opinions or to try to bring you over to his way of thinking, which interviewees sometimes like to do.

Another point you should follow before submitting a column is to check your spelling, as misspellings allow you to lose credibility with the public. Editors don't always catch misspellings. A case in point was when I was a young reporter on a newspaper staff. I wrote an article about a local accordionist and misspelled the word "accordion" throughout. My editor didn't catch the misspelling before it went into print, but my readers sure did. Oh, the phone calls and letters! Even on my weekly trip to the supermarket, I received flack when I ran into a teacher I knew.

In particular, check your spelling of proper names, both first names and surnames. Never assume that someone uses the common spelling for his name. How many times have writers spelled my last name in publications as "DiGregorio," when in fact, I spell it "Digregorio." But, then let's take a more common example that you'll run into: is it Anne or Ann? Is it Teri, Terri, or Terry? Further, if you make references to a famous person or historical figure, check the spelling. It's not uncommon to see even famous people's names misspelled in publications.

And, of course, if you quote a wife and her husband, make sure they have the same surnames.

In writing a column, in general, realize that editors do not want to rewrite poorly-written columns. They have a myriad of duties, including selecting and scheduling which articles to run, coordinating the editorial and photographic and/or graphic art elements, designing pages, and supervising staff writers. At small publications, editors are also busy writing some of their own pieces. Therefore, don't force an editor to reject a good idea for a regular or guest column on the basis of poor writing.

Chapter 3

THE CREATIVE COLUMN

Do you have to be creative to write a creative type of column? I don't think so. You see, there are different types of creative columns. When I say creative column, a bell probably goes off in your head and you think I'm talking solely about the kind where you write about yourself. However, not all of your creative columns need to be personal ones about your daily life. For example, syndicated columnist Bob Greene often writes creative type of columns (reporter-style) which often border on straight feature articles. (The aspect which distinguishes them from straight feature articles is that he is writing them to make a moral point.) For example, Greene writes profiles featuring people he's interviewed that he wants to call the public's attention to for some reason (i.e. a person who struggles with a particular problem such as a homeless person who illustrates the plight of the homeless.) In writing this type of column, a moral point is evident throughout the column and perhaps a clinching, concluding statement is sometimes made. The creative aspect of the column is also evident in the description of the person and the environment in which he functions.

Let's separate the creative types of columns in two broad categories: the highly-personal creative column and the "not-so" personal kind. Let's take the former, first—that is, the most difficult.

Personal Creative Columns

To write this type of creative column is difficult for even professional writers to do on a regular basis. You have to be willing to put a lot about yourself down on paper—how you think, how you feel, and a lot of personal facts about your own life. Your readers, after reading your column over a period of time, will know almost as much about you and your daily life as members of your own family do. This, at times, can get to be a strain on you and your family. Your family may become embarrassed about little revelations of your family life when they glare at them in print, even though you asked permission from them to reveal those little facts. (Oh, they really hit home when they are in print!) And, if you write about yourself, it can get burdensome and weary to analyze your life constantly so that you will have enough material to write about.

When syndicated columnist Anna Quindlen wrote her "Life in the 30's" column, she was skilled at writing a highly-personal column about her daily life. (I've listed one of her books in the appendix which will give you a lot of ideas in this area.) However, Quindlen burned out on this type of column writing and now she writes a less personal type of column called "Public & Private" which is news issue-oriented.

To write creative columns by drawing from your own personal experiences, it's essential to be the type of person who records thoughts as meticulously as one who writes a diary. Always, I mean always, carry a notebook. Even in your car. Keep a notebook in the kitchen, while you're cooking, to record thoughts as they come to you. I almost feel like hanging a notebook around my neck or keeping one dangling from my belt holes like a custodian carries keys.

Analyze every aspect of your own behavior. For example, as an adult, do you still stop at the gum and toy machines at the supermarket and insert a quarter just to see what prize you'll get? Do you know a lot of other people who do this? Have you sat or stood next to a gum or toy machine and watched other adults insert their money? What do these people look like? Do you think they are getting the item for a child? Do you think they're getting it for themselves? If so, is this a sign that there's the child in all adults? Write about this, and give other examples of "the child" who still lurks in you and in adults, in general.

What bothers you about human nature? People's vanity, for example? Examples of people's vanity are heard in everyday conversation. Have you ever stopped to listen and record examples? For example, today I heard a person say that the state I live in, Oregon, is God's country. Strangely, or not so strangely, when I lived in Illinois, I knew people who referred to that state as God's country. Have you ever noticed how many people say that the part of the country they happen to be living in is God's country? Further, have you heard people in your neighborhood say that your school district is the best in the city? Still another example: have you ever noticed that when a lot of people refer to the college they went to, they always say it has the reputation for being one of the best in their particular field? Examples of vanity are all around us. Are you really bothered by vanity? Or do you just accept it in other people? Do you see vanity as part of your nature?

If you're writing a highly-personal creative column, know thyself or seek to know thyself. I once wrote a creative column about how I was a true tightwad. I did this after analyzing how I'd always go to great lengths to save money. For example, even now, I drive down the entire block before I park in a space, just to look for a parking meter that has some leftover time in it. I used to check out all the dryers at the Laundromat to see if there was one with leftover drying time. And, losing money still pains me, even when I lose a nickel in places that are inaccessible, like beneath the car seat. Further, if a waitress tells me that tomato and onions on my burger are 20 cents extra, I pass on them, even though I'd normally have them if they weren't extra. My examples of my "tightwadness" (I can't find the word in my dictionary) were numerous and I attributed my parsimony to being brought up in an ethnic household where thriftiness was taught at a young age. However, I analyzed where I drew the line, and I found that I tended to be generous with others. It annoys me, for example, when people I know send leftover Christmas cards to me from the previous year. (I do have a good memory. At least they could have skipped a year or two.) Besides, I would never do this myself to save money.

After my column ran, readers wrote to me with examples of their tightwadness and this led to a follow-up column on how other tightwads save money. It was a sort of instructional how-to for aspiring tightwads.

In addition, I once wrote a column on pet peeves after someone told me I complain a lot about little things. At this point, I began keeping a pet peeve log over a two-month period, and I broke the log down into various categories, such as pet peeves at the supermarket, at the restaurant, and at the post office.

What are your pet peeves? You can keep a general log and when you collect many pet peeves, you can break them down into categories, too.

Are you bothered by people who give handkerchiefs as gifts? Are you bothered by people who actually use them and wad them back in their pocket or purse? Bothered by people who blow their noses with them one minute and then shake hands with others the next?

What are your other pet peeves? What about in spoken speech? Bothered by people who use complicated words out of context? People who turn verbs into nouns? People who mispronounce words? People who talk "backwards?" (That is, someone who says, for example, "Cooking well does not a chef make" ?) People who tell you to smile, as if that's any of their business? People who, in-between talking, click and pop their gum, instead of just chewing the "dern" thing?

Is rudeness one of your pet peeves? People who notice you're waiting for their parking space and deliberately stall their departure? (Or, they don't signal you on if they're not planning to move.) Jaywalkers who won't even turn their heads to look at you, even though your car is nearly on top of them? (Ouch!)

What about pet peeves at the supermarket? People who get into the express lane and fudge on their number of items? Supermarket checkout clerks who smack your cans against the price scanner and dent them? Clerks who give you one thin bag to hold multiple bottles and cans? Shoppers who abandon their carts in the parking lot, only to have them dent other cars?

What do your pet peeves tell you about yourself? Do you find pet peeves everywhere? In everything that you do? What would a psychologist tell you about yourself? (As if someone with a lot of pet peeves would even care!)

What pet peeves do you have about parents? Your own? The parents of your friends? (Use fictitious names, if you write about them.) The parents you observe? (Don't you just hate parents who keep their toddlers on those chest leashes? I knew a parent who did this. When I was in high school, I always had a high regard for this certain teacher, until one Saturday when I saw her at the supermarket and my eye alarm went off: she was toting her two-year-old on a leash, as if the poor creature were nothing more than her dog.)

What pet peeves do you have about society: the American business world? Companies which bill you and ask you to be a "clerk" besides, that is, by having you record your 12-digit account number on your check when you return payment stub? What else bothers you? Professionals who don't understand professional courtesy—the ones who bill you for every bit of information, even a 10-second phone call requiring a "yes" or "no" answer?

What pet peeves do you have concerning the service sec-

tor of the job world? Do you wish we could go back to the
days when tradespeople were not "artists?" When a hairdresser was not a "hair stylist?" When a gardener was not a
"landscape artist?" When a mechanic was not a "car fixition?"
Thirty years ago, these "artists" were actually affordable.

What pet peeves do you have concerning consumerism
in today's society? Do you wish we could go back to when
as a society we weren't so spoiled? When hospital clinic
lobbies didn't look like living rooms out of some upscale
lifestyle magazine? When hospital birthing rooms weren't
like hotel suites? When parents didn't buy custom-made
clothing for their daughters' dolls? When porcelain toilet
bowls weren't a collector's item? When people didn't eat
gourmet food six days a week?

What pet peeves do you have about the American perspective on youth? Just who thought of those round arbi-
trary numbers which mark old age: 60, 70, 80? Why not
68? 74? 83?

What pet peeves do you have concerning the role of
television in society? Are you tired of the television talk
show trend which focuses on sensational topics? Are you
tired of the broadcast news which gives dignity to con-
victed murderers on death row by interviewing them just
before their execution? And, what does this say about the
media? What does this say about the public who watches
television?

If you don't like writing about pet peeves, maybe you
could write about things you are nostalgic for. For example,
the other day, I went to a rummage sale which had many
items from the 50s and 60s. I was transported back in time.
I saw the suitcase-style portable record players of my childhood, the kind I owned and also the kind from school.
Later, I thought of other items which were a significant
part of my childhood. For example, I remembered the
fresh pink erasers the teacher gave me, the fat pencils I
learned to write with, and the shiny color gummed stars
on school papers which I did well on. Also, I remembered
how I was ashamed to wear homemade clothes to school,

and specifically a green knit sweater my mother made for me which I should have appreciated. Then, I got to wondering how today's kids feel about homemade clothes. (Probably not so bad as I did; in fact, now they are in vogue). If I were to write about nostalgia, I'd write about the simple things which were important to me as a kid, versus what is important to kids today.

Another approach to nostalgia might be a more broad one. Are you a nostalgic person, in general? If so, do you keep momentos from 30 years ago or even those which go back to your childhood which are monetarily worthless? Tell your readers what they are. Do these items say anything about your tastes, or about the things you appreciate in life?

Incidentally, if you are a nostalgic person, read syndicated columnist Russell Baker who includes a lot of nostalgia and sentimentality in his writing. (His anthologies of columns are listed in this book's appendix.) Baker deals a lot with emotions, and he does a good job appealing to the reader's emotions. You can also read syndicated columnist Lewis Grizzard who is adept at expressing nostalgia and his emotions. (Look in the book's appendix for his work, too.)

Along the lines of nostalgia, what little things do you regret? Do you regret having studied literary classics as a college student when, at that time, you knew so little about life and therefore, couldn't really appreciate them? Do you regret having dropped piano lessons as a kid when you thought they were boring? Do you regret not having learned to cook your mother's favorite recipes? How have your tastes changed since you were younger? What do you value now as an adult that you didn't value when you were younger? Build a column around this topic.

As for another column idea, what are you usually ashamed to openly admit? (This could be a humorous column, if you feel you can pull off humor. If not, that's okay.) Have you ever, for example, been jealous of your best friend? In what instances? Have you ever told your husband and kids that you needed them to vacate the house for the afternoon in order to get your work done, when, in fact, after they left, you used the peace and quiet just to sleep? Have you ever told a co-worker who invited you for dinner that you were on a diet and couldn't accept, only to stay home and eat nachos? Do you know other people who have done the same sorts of things? Or, do you think you are atypical? Build a column around this topic.

Tell your readers about your idiosyncrasies. When you see a woman gas station attendant, for example, do you avoid her and drive into the pump station with the male attendant? Have you ever eaten a pasta sandwich instead of a meatball sandwich? Do you think other people have your idiosyncrasies? A column on your idiosyncrasies could be entertaining, and most likely, some readers would automatically write to you to tell you theirs. This could even lead to a follow-up column on idiosyncrasies. You don't need to identify readers by name; initials will do, if readers don't want to be identified.

Do you get the idea about these type of creative columns? In order to write about yourself, you must submit to self-analysis. You must love to share yourself with others: your ideas, likes, dislikes, future plans, and family life, to name just a few. You can't be shy about letting others into your world. How do you feel about your life now, about life in general, about your life in the past? How would you like your life to be? How do you feel about society—how it used to be, how you think it should be?

Ideas come from everywhere. Use your senses. Remember, if you visit the supermarket regularly, record your ideas, thoughts, and complaints about supermarket shopping. If you go to restaurants, regularly record your thoughts about them, too.

Record your thoughts after just driving around the neighborhood. A few weeks ago, I saw a gas station with an Espresso Bar. How ridiculous! Does this tell me anything about society? Or, at least, what does this tell me about the town I live in?

Record your thoughts about going to a hair stylist. Record your complaints. I, for one, am tired of hair stylists using a curling iron to hide the crooked mess they make in cutting my hair. I'm tired of being told that a certain hairstyle won't look good on me just because the stylist probably doesn't know how to do it. Besides, don't you think, as I do, that it's unjust that a hair stylist who spends 15 minutes cutting your hair earns more money per 15 minutes than a lot of professionals do?

Have you been anyplace interesting lately, beyond your daily routine? Have you been to a Marriage Encounter? Did you like it? What went on there? Be detailed. Be specific. What didn't you like about it? If you liked it and benefited from it, give the reasons why. Ask your husband for his opinion, too. Quote him on it. It's also important in a column to give opposing opinions. Give both sides of the issue. If you liked it, try to come up with a couple you met there who didn't like it and who would be willing to be quoted as such in your column.

Wherever you go, as a columnist, you should observe and hear and smell everything, too. Don't take anything for granted. Listen to a dog or cat sighing. Observe how they rest their paws on your lap while they lay beside or on top of you. Experience the joy of having them roll over on their backs and look up at you. Or, if you're standing in back of their heads, watch them look at you with their eyes tilted backward.

Were you driving along in your car today and did you see a dog on the sidewalk who resembled the one you once had as a child? Did that dog look up at you and when he did, was it like seeing your own dog reborn? What childhood memories did that bring back? Do you remember your dog walking you to school? Do you remember your dog waiting with your mother for your return along the school bus route? Write a column about your dog, if you once had one, taking off from this experience of seeing a dog which resembled him.

Today, did a child you didn't know wave to you while your car pulled up in back of the one he was riding in? Did this trigger your memory of when your own kid was small?

Write about this. Or, what does this tell you about children? Their ingenuousness? Do you wish you had the ingenuousness of children?

Have you ever observed the look of pride and vanity on a child's face when you compliment him? You could, as another example, write a column about how as adults, we lose our ingenuousness and become cynical. What experiences of cynicism do you have to share? How do you fight your cynicism?

What thoughts often occupy your mind? Do you read the newspaper often and see articles about murder, illness, or car accidents? Are you troubled by the random nature of life? Write a column about the random nature of life and how you've reconciled yourself to this fact.

What issues in the news bother you? Birth control devices being offered to high schoolers through school clinics? Write a column about this. Or, write a column about an issue such as a law requiring physicians to notify a parent before an abortion is performed on their teen-age daughter (an issue in my state). Personalize the problem. Talk about how you would feel in regards to your own daughter. Whenever you voice an opinion, it is always more interesting to the reader to hear the personal side to it—how it would affect you.

Write a column about an experience you just had, such as your search in finding a suitable baby-sitter, and the problems you ran up against. What did it take to finally find the right one?

As another column idea, what appeared in your mailbox today? Did you receive an interesting advertisement? Or, did you find an interesting flyer or piece of literature left at your doorstep? Did it contain some interesting information or idea which says something about our modern culture which you could build a column around? Did you receive a paid political announcement about a candidate that was more original than the run-of-the-mill kind you've gotten before?

Save what you get in the mail or on your doorstep, even

if there's only a remote possibility that you'll, at some point, use it. Maybe later on, after you've collected different pieces of mail or literature, you'll see a pattern of ideas emerge from them. I've seen a pattern to the advertisements I get in the mail. It seems that no matter what kind of product someone is trying to sell me, the advertiser is trying to appeal to my need to make money, look younger, feel healthier, be more sexy, or improve myself in some way. So, be a collector of all printed material, and store them into certain files: (i.e. advertisement file.)

I always seem to receive materials in the mail from local colleges and graduate schools, which, in needing funds, offer half-baked degree programs requiring little or no work for adult students. It seems incredible to me, as they claim, that you can hold down a 40-hour a week job, raise a family, and go to school. I'd like to write a column about this, recounting my own demanding experience as a student.

Did you receive a phone call recently with a recorded message? Did you follow-up the call with a call to investigate the offer? (If you're a columnist, you should have, because you should be constantly looking for column ideas.) Was it a funny offer? How did you feel—imposed upon? When you followed up, did you ask how they got your number? Did you ask them how you could get off their list? Report on your findings. Do you often feel that your privacy is being invaded? What are some other instances when you've felt this way?

Analyze yourself, despite the fact that this can get really draining after a period of time. Do you enter contests for prizes you don't want, just to see if you'll win? I do this constantly. Though, I have no kids, I entered a contest to win a dollhouse. I also recently entered a contest to see if I could win a living room set that I don't even have room for. Do you know a lot of other people who do this, too? What does this say about you? Or, does this say something about human nature, in general?

Remember, when you write a highly-personal creative

column, you must be able to put into words emotions and ideas which others have, but which they don't know how to express. As I've said, Anna Quindlen, syndicated columnist and staffer of *The New York Times*, wrote a very popular personal type of column about daily life some years back with the logo "Life in the 30's." She incorporated her innermost perspectives on her own personal life with skill, dealing with marriage and family, among other issues. When I reread the columns Quindlen wrote, I often think, "If only a man could write Anna Quindlen type of columns from a male perspective on his own personal life, what a success he'd be."

Non-Personal Creative Columns:

The Columnist As Reporter

If you're not inclined to getting too introspective, you can write creative columns which lean more toward reporting on things around you. For example, you can write about common or unusual incidents or events, trends of the decade, and changing lifestyles by focusing on other people who are involved in these or who illustrate them.

As a columnist-reporter, you must be active, always seeking out new activities or places. For example, go to a big-time wrestling show and observe the theatrics—report on them. Report on the sounds, for example, and all the words flying around, not only from the wrestler-performers, but from the spectators, too.

As a columnist, you cannot just report on someone or something which is interesting, but you are trying to make a point about some aspect of life or an issue. Further, it must be clear to the reader why you chose to report on such a topic. For example, what is big-time wrestling all about? Tell the person you're sitting next to at the show that you're a writer and that you'd like a quote from him about why he went to the show. What does he enjoy about big-time wrestling? What does he think others enjoy about it? Get a quote from the referee and coaches. Ask the coaches if they can call the wrestlers over to you for comments. Tell everyone you're a writer.

Tell your readers what happens at such a show, about some of the more colorful moves of the wrestlers. Of course, give your opinion on the show. What types of people go to these shows? What do you think of the wrestlers? If you were a straight news reporter, your opinion wouldn't count, but as a columnist-reporter, your opinion is certainly crucial to the column.

As a columnist, when you are reporting on something, you need to be a good observer. So, sharpen your observation skills, and in turn, you'll become skilled at describing details. Practice observing and describing what you observe, as a routine. At the wrestling show, what are the typical movements on the part of the wrestlers? What do the coaches do? What does the referee do? What does he say? From your observation and description, you want your readers to feel like they were actually there.

Remember, description is of vital importance. Take in the physical surroundings. For example, what is the arena of the wrestling match like? Take in as much as you can about the spectator area. Are all the seats filled? Find out what the seating capacity is and approximate how many people there are, or ask the ticket-taker. Observe, that is, have a camera-eye. Besides the sights and sounds of the spectators and wrestlers, describe how the place smells. Pretend you are describing the action and scene to a blind person, the sounds to a deaf person, and the smell to someone who has lost his sense of smell.

Whenever you go to places you often visit, or new places or events, think in terms of getting a column out of them. For example, what goes on at garage sales, if you normally go to them? Do you have a friend who holds garage sales often? If so, go to her garage sale. Quote her on any unusual things that happen at garage sales. Ask her what is the most unusual item that someone has ever come looking for? Observe the bargain hunters. What trinkets are most popular with them? What do you notice about human nature at a garage sale? What do you like about garage sales and/or dislike about them? Would you want to hold one? What would you advise your readers about how to hold a garage sale? How should items be priced? What would you warn them about garage sales? What items don't seem to sell? What was the strangest item your friend had on sale?

As a columnist-reporter of creative columns, you must observe or participate in as many different things as you can in the community. Why not, for example, take an adult evening class or a one-evening workshop at a community college? Then, you could write about an offbeat or interesting workshop you've participated in or visited. (By the way, as a columnist, you could probably attend free of charge if you received the permission of the school's adult education supervisor.) Scan class catalogues, and you'll find workshops given by speech coaches, for example. Write about the workshop by observing what goes on and your impressions of the interaction. Get quotes from the speech coach and those from the attendees about why they want to be trained in communicating well. What is your opinion of the workshop? What did you learn? Tell your readers.

Community college extension workshops are often taught by noted professionals in the community, and attending these would provide you with not only ideas for interesting columns, but you would make important contacts for information on topics for future columns. Or, you could even come up with an interesting teacher to profile in your column, not focusing on his teaching, but on his professional nine to five job.

You can often write creative columns of a profile nature by keeping a list of interesting people to interview as you hear, read about them, or as they come to you through your contacts. As I've said before, keep a list of all names, even though you may decide to delete some of these possibilities at a later time. When you interview an interesting person, never forget to include interesting tidbits you've gathered from the interview. For example, was the judge you interviewed an ex-cop? Was the science fiction author you interviewed once a failure in high school science courses?

For a profile type of column, you might, for example, write about a young mother for a Mother's Day column—one woman who has chosen motherhood over a career. In this column, you could relay her opinions, perspectives, and background. Was she once a professional woman, or did she get married and have children right out of school? Does she know many other women like herself, ones who've chosen the same path? Does she live a lot like her mother did? What's different about how she lives and the way her mother did? In this column, you should leave the reader with a sense of what it's like to devote oneself full-time to motherhood in a modern society which has so many attractive options for women out in the job world. You should also let your reader know about what you think of this woman and if you feel you could live the same sort of life she does.

Incidentally, today I saw the bumper sticker "motherhood is a proud profession." (Hint: Keep your eyes open for bumper stickers which you can build a column around.)

Let me give you another example of a profile column. I once wrote a column around the Christmas season about a Salvation Army bell ringer and her view of helping the needy. I decided to interview her after seeing her stationed on the same street corner for about three consecutive years during the holidays. I reported not only on her background as a social worker, but on her childhood and religious upbringing which led her to her present charitable attitudes. I interviewed her about her view of modern day society. Besides quoting the interviewee, I also got a direct quote about her generosity from another Salvation Army worker who knew her well. (I had asked the bell ringer for the name of someone she knew well from the Salvation Army.) Recognize that whenever you do a profile column, you can get quotes from others who know the person, if you feel they are relevant. I concluded my column with my perspective of this woman and my feeling that everyone needs to meet more people like her because she makes us realize that focusing on others is much more rewarding than focusing on ourselves.

In doing a profile column, you must go prepared to interview that person. You must have a list of questions in hand to ask your interviewee. Go prepared with your questions written in a stenographer's notebook. (I do not tape interviews because I feel tape recorders tend to force people to come up with answers quickly, without giving them time to reflect. I try to allow for a casual and relaxed visit, with a minimal amount of pressure on the interviewee. Besides, tape recorders sometimes malfunction and the interview is then lost.) For a profile column, you can spend even a couple of hours talking to the interviewee. Just make sure that when you call to schedule the interview or visit, you indicate about how much time you'd like to spend talking with him. I find that an interview can run lengthily, particularly if you're interviewing someone with an interesting hobby. In this case, you would want to observe the person doing his hobby, so you could report to the reader about it.

For a profile column, you should ask about 20 questions to the interviewee, covering all relevant details including his background. For example, if you're interviewing someone with an interesting job or hobby, you'll want to tell your reader how he got started doing what he does, and what he did before. You will want to relay to the reader why you have singled out this person to write about, and what is significant about what he does, or what he offers as a lesson or example to us.

When interviewing someone and taking notes, create your own shorthand of abbreviations. If the interviewee speaks too fast, ask him to slow down or repeat something. If his answers are vague, ask for a clarification. Remember to ask "how" or "why" to get him to give you more specific answers, rather than just a "yes" or "no" response. Or, if you're not sure you understand a response, say to him, "Do you mean to say that..."

Besides your prepared questions, be open, of course, to seeing and listening to whatever else comes up during the interview. However, if the interviewee digresses too much, tell him politely that you'd like to further pursue a different area. At the end of the interview, ask the interviewee if he'd like to add any comments which your questions didn't lead to.

For profile columns, interesting people are all around you. Have you seen a regular street corner musician who, over a period of six months, plays daily, eight hours a day? Have you ever thought of interviewing him? What's his background? Why does he do this? How much does he make? These questions should be asked, and you should also give your impressions of the guy.

Do you know a veterinarian who treats zoo animals, for example, and who seems to spend more time around animals than people? If not, ask about one at the zoo. Contact its public relations person and tell him that you're a writer who'd like to interview one of their veterinarians. For a column, I once interviewed a zoo veterinarian. I asked him how he viewed human nature after working around animals, what he liked and disliked about his job, and if he enjoyed being around animals more than people. I went out on his rounds with him one day and observed what he did, how he dealt with the animals, and what he said to them. Remember the song, "Talk to the Animals"? I observed how this veterinarian talked to the animals and how they responded to him. I also observed how he dealt with some of the more exotic animals and reported on this. The moral of this column was along the lines of how some of us march to the beat of a different drummer.

As another idea, you could write a profile column about

a person who lives an extraordinarily opulent lifestyle. Everyone loves to read these profiles. I had once saved an article I clipped from the newspaper about a lottery winner. A few years after this person won the lottery, I decided to write about him and update the public on how he was doing, and of course, what he was doing with all his money. (I tracked him down through a former neighbor of his.) If you interview such a person, be thorough in your reporting. How is his lifestyle opulent? Was the door answered by a butler? (Of course, you are to visit him in his "environment.") Does this person have a home with llama rugs? Recreate, for the reader, the scene by using as much detail as possible. Does he own an expensive breed of dog? Were the walls painted purple or wall-papered in an exotic pattern? Ask this person how his life has changed since he became rich. Is he having trouble thinking of ways to spend his money? Is he donating money to charities? Which charities? How is his life happier? What are the negative aspects of being rich? Are strangers always contacting him, asking for money? What kinds of crackpots have contacted him with requests? Are salespeople always trying to sell him something? What kind of salespeople? And, what are some of the more offbeat sales calls he's gotten?

In a profile column, report on anything about this person which is relevant. How does this person walk, talk, and carry himself? Is his hair cropped short? What about his hand gestures? Describe his clothes, if relevant. Describe his physical characteristics. Does he wear a Rolex watch? Diamond rings? Can he be seen driving around town in an expensive convertible? What kind? What places does he frequent? What are his hobbies? How does he spend his Sundays?

As a columnist-reporter, you must ask as many questions as you can. Obviously, not all the answers you get will be interesting, so you won't be including everything in your column, nor will you have space for everything. Focus on relevant facts and curious tidbits. Focus on why this person is important to your readers. What is he an example of?

Why is he significant? Is he an example of a successful person? A spendthrift? A courageous person? What do you think of him?

Besides the profile column, you can write a non-personal creative column by being an observer. Often, columnists go to public places to observe both uncommon and common people. They listen in on private conversations on the bench of a shopping mall or even strike up conversations with strangers. (Of course, use your discretion in this latter instance.) In this latter case, you couldn't be taking notes while talking to the stranger because you'd want the conversation to be as natural as possible. Therefore, you'd have to have a good enough memory to hold off on note-taking until after the stranger had left. You could, for example, strike up a conversation with a typical homemaker at the mall, one with her children, to give your reader an insight into a typical homemaker's life.

As far as listening in on two people with an interesting conversation going, you should often read syndicated columnists Bob Greene and Mike Royko of *The Chicago Tribune* to catch on to the way they do it. They are good observers of people in public places. For example, they listen in on conversations at bars. They report dialogue to personalize the "story," thereby recreating the situation for the reader and breaking up what might otherwise be monotonous narrative. In reporting direct quotes, after all, the reader gets involved and feels as if he is present and watching. Further, dialogue often lends a brisk, lively beat to the column.

What do you see in the person you observe? Do you see a part of yourself? Someone whom you could become like someday? Someone whom you wouldn't like to be like? Do you see in him a part of what a lot of people are like? Or, do you see in him a part of what a lot of people would like to be like? Or, what a lot of people are fearful of becoming?

Observe, observe, observe in public places. If you're driving along and see someone unusual, such as a person dressed up in a costume on a street corner, stop the car, get out, investigate. There may be a column idea in it.

When you're in a parking lot, observe. Isn't it curious, for example, how people who own expensive convertibles park them with the hood down, while people with "junkers" lock them up tight? As a columnist, ask people— people you know, perhaps— why they don't lock up their expensive cars. Ask them what their rationale is. Ask them if they lock the doors of their home. If so, what's the difference in their mind? And, what's your view on this topic? Further, ask a police officer if the police station often gets vandalism reports about expensive convertibles left wide open. What is the police officer's perspective on this? Build a column around this topic.

As far as other public places to observe in, have you ever been to a bus station? Have you ever noticed how women who are alone in bus stations often head to the pay phone and pretend they are talking to someone to avoid being hassled by men? Or, they stand near a vendor—anything, so they don't have to sit and wait alone. What else can you observe at bus stations? I would imagine a good column could be written from observing at a bus, train, or subway station.

Sharpen your observation skills at all times. For example, observe an old person walking along, then try to describe this. Does he keep his eyes straight ahead, to the ground, or on passersby while clutching belongings?

Talk to everyone: the household repairman, your mechanic, your plumber. Everyone has something interesting to say or to inform you about, if you really listen. My mechanic told me that his primary worry was about what his children would grow up to be like, given the influence of gangs in the school system. Is there a gang problem at your kids' school? Maybe this could be a topic for your column. Or, on a lighter and brighter note, are the kids in your school district doing something constructive for the community, such as starting a project to raise money for the needy or helping the elderly with work around their homes? If so, write a column about this. You might write in your lead sentence something like: "With all the negativity going around about today's kids, some local kids are deserving of commendation, being involved in constructive projects." Your column would include direct quotes from the kids about the project, a direct quote from their teacher-supervisor, and some quotes from the people they are helping. You could make your point, for example, about how keeping kids busy, keeps them out of trouble.

As another column idea, take a current issue like homelessness and write a column illustrating it by focusing on one homeless person. Scour the streets and interview one whom you find to be interesting. For confidentiality, you could refer to him by his first name or by a fictitious first name. (In the latter case, tell your reader it's a fictitious name.) Prepare a list of extensive questions (at least 20) before you hit the streets. When you find the homeless person, tell him you'd like to interview him for a column. Among other questions, ask how he became homeless, how long he's been homeless, what his life is like now, in contrast to what it used to be like when he wasn't homeless, and what his typical day is like. Of course, describe his physical appearance and his dress.

I have another note on writing about issues. Use fictitious names only when necessary. I've seen many freelancers use fictitious names too haphazardly. Use fictitious names to protect identity on confidential topics. For example, if you're writing a column on the difficulties of losing weight, and as an example, you want to interview someone who has lost 200 pounds, but he doesn't want you to reveal his identity, then try, instead, to come up with someone else who will go on record. You see, giving someone's real name really allows the problem to hit home with the reader. It gives the problem "a face." Confidentiality, in the case of the overweight person, isn't usually that crucial. It is, however, necessary where real stigma is involved such as in the case of a homeless person.

Let's take another issue for a column, such as a child stricken by a rare disease, one whose parents can't afford to pay medical bills for. If you are writing about a topic such as this, your goal will be to bring public attention to the plight of the poor and the cost of medical care, perhaps even to make a case for a national health care system. If the relatives of this child are trying to raise funds for him, you can mention that a fund is being established at a bank to where people can make donations.

Incidentally, once you've established yourself as a regular columnist, the public will often approach you with such topics and examples of specific people to write about, in care of the publication you write for.

As far as other issues to write about, a recent issue in my state was whether the law should require seatbelt usage in cars. If I'd written a column about this, I would have found a person to interview who wasn't wearing a seatbelt when he was involved in a car accident which left him a paraplegic. How would I have found such a person, you ask? I would have contacted the committee or group in favor of putting this measure on the ballot, and most likely it would have known of someone like this.

As for writing about issues, I'd like to cover one last point. If you are writing on your opinion about a national issue, and your column is for a local audience, "localize" the opinion. That is, be sure to include local examples of that national issue. Let's take an example of what I mean. If you are writing about how you feel that women in broadcasting are cast aside when they reach middle age (a commonly-held view), don't just give examples of nationally-famous women in broadcasting; get comments and quotes from local women who are in broadcasting, or who once were, but who were encouraged to leave when they got older. In addition, to give both sides of the issue, quote a local manager of a television station who refutes this idea.

In your creative columns, you could also give information on leisure activities available in town or even places you've discovered where consumers can go to a problem resolved. Remember, if you're writing your column and you want readers to perceive you as their friend, there's really no limit to what you can do or cover in your column.

In Summary

The good thing, therefore, about a creative column, in general, is that it can be a catchall that can deal with a potpourri of topics and issues. Always make a practice of reading newspaper ads, and newsletters and brochures put out by local organizations, such as the public library (to discover local groups or organizations). Also read billboard signs and ads in the phone book's Yellow Pages. What do these tell you about trends and lifestyles? Look for common themes running though various media. Read alumni magazines to find out about changes that have occurred since you were of college age. (You could write a column on how college life has changed since you were in school.)

Read news releases in local publications and in newsletters of organizations. You may want to attend community events and meetings of organizations to report on them. In the latter case, you could write about your impressions on what certain organizations do and how they can help the public. Also read press releases in newspapers and magazines about local special interest groups which are springing up. You may want to attend their meetings. (If so, contact the group's leader and let him know you're coming to meet him and to talk to him and the members.) Or, write about a group you're connected with.

For other ideas, read columnists in other parts of the country who write creative columns.

Get the idea? Ideas are all around you. I bet all these years you've probably wondered how "those columnists get all their ideas to keep writing about." It's no secret. They are no different than anyone else. They just read a lot and keep their eyes and ears open at all times. You do exactly the same!

What about the gossip column? (Many people consider this to be under the category of creative column.) As a gossip columnist, you could focus on social happenings and the movers and shakers in town. For this type of column, you would obviously have to cultivate a lot of sources and be willing to spend a lot of time on the telephone verifying tidbits of information. Caution: don't believe anything—let alone print anything—until you do verify them. I once worked in a newsroom in the Midwest next to a reporter who kept a sign on his desk with a lot of wisdom behind it: "If your mother says she loves you, check it out." Gossip columnists (and other columnists, too) take heed! Here again, be careful about libel.

Taking A Closer Look At Creative Columns

Following is a (fabricated) creative column with basic journalistic problems. As before, read the column using the basic criteria which you know for judging it, such as content and style. Make notes to yourself about the column's deficiencies. Once again, before reading the commentary, number each paragraph (including all indentations) to be able to follow it.

This is the column:

I've reached another milestone in my life. On June 11, I'll be celebrating the 40th anniversary of my college graduation. Where have all the years gone? My class will have a reunion just as it has had every ten years since. I've been to each one.

As I think about the past reunions I've attended, I've formulated some answers to the following questions: (1) What kinds of reunions are there? (2) Who arranges reunions? (3) Why do people attend reunions?

There must be as many kinds of reunions as there are kinds of groups or organizations. But, most reunions can be grouped into basic classifications: family reunions, war veterans' reunions, and high school and college reunions.

Although I've never been to a family reunion because I come from a small family, I've always been curious as to what goes on at them, and each year I devour accounts of them in the society columns of weekly community newspapers. (I guess deep down, I've always wished I'd come from a large family or married into one.) From what I've read, these reunions are very organized—in fact, the detail that goes into them is astounding. They are as well-planned as large weddings. Every year, a new committee is formed to arrange for the next year's bash. They all seem to be held outdoors in the summer with a barbecue.

Usually, those attending the family reunions are all known to each other with the exception of newlyweds and the "infant" additions to the family. The program consists of a master of ceremony who gives the opening speech in a humorous fashion. He identifies the oldest family member, the oldest family-returnee, the couple that has been married the longest, the family which has traveled the farthest, the family with the most children, and the couple with the most grandchildren. He also makes mention of those unable to attend.

I can imagine that after each of the above identifications, there is a round of hearty applause, hoops and hollers, some red faces, or even some tears.

As far as veterans' reunions, I know nothing of them.

Who arranges reunions? The school reunions I've attended have always been arranged by women. The committee has men on it, because males were predominately the class officers in those days. But, I have never known men to be the major organizers of the reunion.

As far as who attends, curiosity is obviously a primary motive, especially in my case, as I like to see old friends, whom were it not for these reunions, I would only be able to keep in touch with through long distance calls and letters. (Incidentally, I'm a poor letter-writer.) People, in general, like to reminisce with their old friends, but beyond that, they are curious to see who has aged more quickly, whom life has treated more kindly (familywise and jobwise) and who has had the most ups and downs in life, in general.

As for the school reunion site, people love to walk on campus grounds and in buildings. Although with the passing of each ten years, there have undoubtedly been changes, renovations, and alterations in land-scaping and buildings on site, most of the old sites are still there. And, you feel like you're walking back into the past, reliving your thoughts, feelings, fears, and once-future hopes during those youthful days. Your present concerns and the "life-battering" that have occurred in the past decades are momentarily erased as you are emersed in your youthful innocence.

Getting back to who attends, I am certain about one thing: people who have failed in life do not attend. It's the successful people or at least the people who fared well financially who come.

Single people—those who've just gotten divorced or separated—often attend and waste no time letting people know they are unattached and "looking." They relish the hope that they'll meet other singles or that their old friends will file away this information for future reference. Who knows, they think, maybe in the future their old friends may get divorced or they may be able to introduce them to a single relative or another single friend.

Another thing I've noticed about attendees is that people never seem to change personalitywise. The people whom I long ago labeled as jerks are still jerks. Their circumstances may have changed, but their underlying personality is still alive and well, thank you. Conversely, the people who seemed to be nice and humble, still are.

However, what changes in people are the physical transformations which, at first sight, take others by surprise. The people who were overweight and who used to constantly battle the fat, are now the svelte types who show no evidence of their former struggles. It's now their turn in life to be the beautiful and handsome ones. And what about the former homecoming queens and the handsome student body presidents? At reunions, they show up as the bedraggled homemakers and the not-so gracefully-aged men, respectively. These homecoming queens never married the successful men they seemed destined to. And, the student body presidents which the yearbook editors touted as "the most likely to succeed"—well, all they achieved was professional mediocrity.

I wonder what other gems of wisdom I'll return with after this next reunion. I just may come away with more insight into the ironies of life.

Commentary

In general, this column has many problems. The column is lacking in major ways in that it really doesn't offer specifics in personal experiences, observations, or references to individuals. For example, we never find out any specific experiences the writer had while attending prior school reunions. The writer could have referred to people by using fictitious names (and telling her readers that she did that), thereby not making identifications which would embarrass individuals. The writer doesn't even name the college buildings and sites she revisited to bring the story to life. Did she, for example, used to hang out at the student union and how has this changed physically, and how are the students who now frequent it different these days? The writer never tells you what her thoughts and fears were as a college student, contrasted with what they are today. Just from my own experience, I know that some of the things I feared would happen after I left college, never did.

Likewise, I wonder what this columnist feared when she was in college and how, in fact, her later life actually turned out. One would expect a college reunion column to essentially be "a walk down memory lane," a nostalgic type of piece. Yet, we find none of that here. The columnist writes like she's producing an English composition on reunions. She bores the reader and sidetracks him by talking about reunions in general, before getting to what we think was supposed to be the heart of the matter: her college reunions.

This columnist defies one of the basic principles of journalism: write by giving examples. The writer could have, for instance, given us examples of some of the successful people who attended the reunion—what they were like in college and what they do now. And, so as not to embarrass (or even libel) the "jerks" and the people whose lives took a turn for the worse, she, of course, would have to deal in very general terms, here.

Another thing that bothers us about this column is the columnist's lack of personal insight. For example, have you ever seen someone again after a few decades and instinctively you knew who they were? This happens to most of us. Did it happen to this columnist? We don't know.

If this columnist couldn't remember specifics from the prior reunions she'd been to, why didn't she postpone writing this column until after she'd gotten back from this new reunion?

If this column had offered personal insights and some specific examples, it would have come to life and become interesting and colorful to the reader. In this type of column, the reader's nostalgia should have been ignited.

Let's examine the details, paragraph by paragraph.

Paragraph 1. This lead paragraph is sufficient, and it does draw the reader into the story. People are naturally curious to read about such a topic, whether or not they've ever attended a reunion. However, "where have all the years gone" is trite and should be omitted.

Paragraphs 2 & 3. These paragraphs are irrelevant. In

the first paragraph, we were led to believe this was a piece about the columnist's school reunion. Now, we are sidetracked with other information. Besides, the statements about the different types of reunions are unnecessary because we all know about these anyway. As far as who arranges reunions and who attends, she could have told us that now, instead of merely posing the questions.

Paragraphs 4, 5, 6, & 7. These paragraphs are also irrelevant. Here, she's talking about reunions which are foreign to her realm of experience. Instead of sidetracking us with reunions which she knows nothing about, she should tell us about her school reunion that she does know about firsthand. The reader asks,"Why isn't she telling me about her school reunions, as she told me she would in Paragraph 1?" (Further, if she really wanted to discuss reunions, in general, including family reunions, she should have told us this in paragraph 1. And, instead of regurgitating generalities about what she's read in newspapers about family reunions, she could have asked friends and acquaintances who could offer specific accounts. She gives us absolutely no details about family reunions. In addition, in paragraph 7, she does what a lot of beginning writers do—she brings up a topic (war veterans' reunions), and never discusses it. If she knows nothing of this type of reunion, she should never have mentioned it. By the way, if paragraph 7 had been relevant, a one-sentence paragraph would have been acceptable in journalistic style. For example, you can use a one-sentence paragraph if you feel the information should stand out or if you want a new paragraph to signal that you've changed the topic.)

Paragraph 8. This is fine.

Paragraph 9. Here, specific examples of old friends should have been given, along with descriptions of who they are, where they live, and what they do.

Paragraph 10. First of all, this paragraph is out of order, because as you later see, paragraph 11 gets back to discussing who attends. Paragraph 10 could have come later, after all the discussion of attendees. As far as content in paragraph 10, basic facts are missing. If she didn't want to give the name of the college to protect the identity of individuals mentioned, she could have discussed its geographic location and the changes her college has undergone. What were her favorite spots on campus when she was a student? Were they still the same on her last visit? Here, her previous reunion experiences of walking on campus could have been discussed. What thoughts did she relive? For example, when she was a college student, what did she think her future occupation would be? Were her professional goals finally realized? Or, did she go into a completely different field than what she had planned? And, here her experiences of life-battering during the past 40 years should be specified to give a personal tone to the column.

Paragraph 11. The reader wonders if she's talking off the top of her head. Can't she give any specific examples of the successful people, such as who they are and what they do for a living?

Paragraph 12. She could be more specific without identifying these single people. Could she recount any conversations she overheard?

Paragraph 13. Here, too, she could be more specific without identifying people. For example, she could give examples of how these jerks acted at the reunion and what they used to do as college students. She could also give examples of the nice people.

Paragraph 14. Perhaps here, too, more specific examples could be given without identifying people. For example, what kind of clothes did the fat people wear back in college? What kind were they wearing as thin people at the last reunion? Even though she didn't give the names of the homecoming queens and student body presidents whose lives had gone bad, it seems that this columnist is getting too specific with mention of them, and the tone of this is mean-spirited! She sounds almost as if she's gloating over the fact that their lives went bad. If she wanted to make a point about the vagaries of life, she could have done it with some taste and compassion!

Paragraph 15. I'd hardly call her comments "gems of wisdom." She shows, at the very least, insensitivity toward those whose lives have gone bad and perhaps, she even shows a sense of satisfaction.

To conclude, the columnist should have written this piece after the reunion to have made it more interesting. She wrote her piece without any personal insights, as if she was writing for an encyclopedia. Later, her column was reduced to some petty, personal comments.

Another Sample Column

This next column is also fabricated. Often, as you know, humorous columns involve the retelling of personal experiences, as this one does. Read the following, but do not bother to number its paragraphs, as we will discuss the column in general terms.

This is the column:

"The adventure of dining out," as we read in restaurant advertisements. It's more likely you've experienced a misadventure in dining out lately. I can't remember the last time I had good food and good service at an affordable price.

Fresh cream for the coffee?

Come on, I tell myself. Use some initiative, and some elbow grease, and tear open those little plastic "thimbles" without spilling that fake stuff labeled "cream." I'll just dare myself to.

More hot water for my tea?

"Gladly," I imagine the waitress saying.

But a fresh tea bag, too? I would never have the courage to ask.

A few restaurant visits ago, I thought I'd discovered some new exotic tea flavor, rather than Lipton, the old standby. But, no, no wait a minute. Hmmm, the rinser-mechanism on the dishwasher must have been on the fritz and given my tea a new twist.

What about the food?

Now, at restaurants, we have gourmet prices for the "luxury" of army surplus food. What was once simple, inexpensive pasta—that you would eat at home the last few days of the month when you were running short on your budget—has become a feast to drain your budget. Imagine, the dressed up spaghetti with real butter and real cream "sauce," with bacon bits too! Ah, a real delicacy from Bologna, Italy. At least, that's what you're told you're paying for, though the Italians wouldn't be so stupid to pay handsomely for this.

I guess it beats the tomato-ketchup sauce—with peripheral water which clung to the side of the dish—that used to top spaghetti when we dined out before this era of the "discriminating diner."

It seems that all we've discriminated ourselves into, is being taken advantage of by restaurant owners.

I joked with Mom during our recent night out. "Hey, lighten up, pasta is a bargain at $30 a plate," I said.

"And how about $20 for a salad with delectable-looking crunchy Chinese noodle things?" Mom asked.

"Oh, I think I'll pass that one up," I said. "Looks like something Teddy whipped up for himself out of desperation when I left on a shopping trip and never came back. He needed something to tide himself over, so who can blame him for that?"

"What's this on the menu?" Mom asked. "Is this really $25 for a green salad with tomatoes, olives, and mushrooms?... Oh, I see the tomatoes are from Provence... Actually, who cares and who can tell the difference... and where is that anyway?"

"Hush, here comes the waitress," I muttered.

"Hi, my name is Cindy, and I'll be your waitress. "

I was tempted to respond, "Hi, my name is Sue, and I'll be your customer," but I bit my tongue after the word "my."

"What's the soup of the day?" Mom quickly intervened as a buffer to my impending snide remark.

"The soup du jour?" the waitress corrected her. "That's a good question. I dunno 'cause I just got here. I'll check."

"Oh, before you check on the soup, the air conditioning is going full blast," I said. "Could it be turned down?"

"Nope, sorry, can't be regulated. Has a mind of its own," the waitress chortled.

"Naturally," I mumbled.

I began to fidget with my silverware, having nothing else to do.

"My goodness, Mom, look at this." I held up my spoon and fork. "Am I getting cataracts at 40, or is the silverware stained?"

Mom took it from my grasp, looked closely at it, and frowned.

"Oh, Miss, Miss, one more thing," I raised my voice as she exited. "May I have another set of silverware? Seems to be a little on the cloudy side," I said, as I held up my silverware, while people at the nearby tables turned to look.

The waitress trudged over to inspect the silverware firsthand. "Hmmm," she said as she examined first the fork, then the spoon. "Yes, does look spotty," she acquiesced. "I'll get you a new set, pronto."

She walked over to the nearby counter, returned, and said, "Do these look any better, Ma'am?"

I looked and said, "Well... a tad less spotted, I suppose." I half-smiled, took a deep breath, shoved the silverware aside, and read the menu.

"Mom, do you know what the specialty is here?"

"Those two ladies across from us are having pasta with curry sauce—it looks like," Mom said. "Oh my, they don't seem to be the type to be in need of such food. They're 'well-over' as it is."

"Oh, give them a break," I said, as I gestured. "After all, they've probably ordered diet pop to compensate for the pasta calories. Overweight people always do make those little token gestures."

"Will you look at that man behind you?" Mom changed the subject. "His coleslaw is swimming in mayonnaise. I wonder if he likes it like that? Yick! ... Listen... he just told his waitress to smile, and she's giving him a toothy grin. He's saying, 'That's much better.' God, what a creep! Being a customer doesn't give him the power to change someone's demeanor."

Our waitress came back.

"The soup is alfalfa. Would you like to order it?"

(Gulp.) "I guess—if that's all you have as the special... How about you, Mom?"

"I guess I'll try it, too."

"And, I'll also have a hamburger," I said.

"And, what will your mother have?"

"I don't know," I said. Then I mumbled: "Why don't you ask her? She's sitting right there."

"I'll have a burger, too," Mom interrupted.

"And, what to drink?"

"Water for both of us," I said,

"You don't want a bottomless glass of pop?" the waitress asked in surprise. "It's only $3. "

"Water, just water," I replied.

"Okay, be right back," the waitress said as she hurried off.

"Mom, did you hear how she pulled the old invisible-elderly person routine?— 'And what will your mother have?' she asked me. "As if you weren't really there, or were too feeble to tell her what you wanted!"

"By now, I'm used to that at restaurants," Mom conceded. "But why can't they automatically serve water?" Mom said shaking her head. "Why do we have to ask for it? Are we in the middle of a drought?"

"That's obvious!" I shot back. "They want you to order pop at $3 with free refills. Only most people don't want the refills, so the customers don't get their money's worth," I said with a snicker. "Makes you want to bring a thermos to carry home the refills you paid for."

Mom ignored my diatribe. "That 'coleslaw man' is complaining to his wife about how he just got a cold baked potato," she remarked. "Now, he's saying that the butter, sour cream, and chive tray doesn't have a serving spoon."

"He'd better watch out," I said. "His waitress looks like she's ready to scoop up the butter, sour cream, and chive tray from him and pass it along to another customer, and he hasn't even touched them yet... Why look at that body language! He's hovering over the tray as she comes by, so she won't snatch it from him."

"Speaking of waitresses," Mom said, "does it take that long to get us soup? It's probably from the can anyway, with some sprouts thrown in."

I spotted the waitress. "Look, over there, Mom," I said as I pointed. "She's bussing that dirty table... the dirty smudged glasses, the dirty wadded up napkins. Yick, what a mess. After that, she'll be delivering our soup and burgers... Oooh! "

"Yum," Mom gasped.

"Look, those people who came in after us and ordered after us, are already well into their entree," I said.

"Get the waitress's attention, now," Mom urged.

"How can I? We've been seated facing the wall," I explained.

"Just pivot like one of those pulsating statues that people put in their front yards at Christmas," she said. "You'll burn some calories in the process, too."

"What's there to burn? I haven't eaten anything yet ... Oh, all right, I will...The waitress didn't see me gesturing. She has tunnel vision."

"There's a lot of that going around with waitresses," Mom said in disgust.

"I'm really getting hungry," I said. "The person in the next booth is champing chips to the beat of the music—dinner à la Muzak, and it's making me nervous and more hungry."

To divert my attention from my hunger, Mom asked, "What's that other waitress doing? Is that supposed to be the main entertainment: rug sweeping for our viewing pleasure?"

"I don't even want to look. Let's change the subject ...Those people who came in after us, who got served a long time ago, have already finished. In fact, they've already gotten their toothpicks out."

Mom frowned. "Handing out toothpicks should be outlawed."

I shook my head. "I've even seen patrons come prepared with ones stashed in their purses and coat pockets."

Mom looked startled. "Our waitress is coming our way without food. Get her attention, quick! "

I motioned to her. The waitress came closer, actually making eye contact.

"Here's your check. You can pay me when you're ready."

"What?" I exclaimed. "We haven't even gotten our soup!"

"Oops, wrong table," the waitress said with a sheepish look. "Don't worry, I'll get your food." She looked closer at the check as she walked over to the next patron's table, mumbling to herself, "Uh, oh, two plus three doesn't equal six."

"Forget it," I said to Mom. "We've taken in all the 'fine dining' we need for one day. Let's get our coats."

We snapped up our purses and walked in haste to the coat rack.

"God, they've been lifted."

Commentary

A creative column of this kind involves a fair amount of work. The writer is recreating a personal experience, and she must recall observations and conversation in detail and then pick out which are the most relevant to include in her story. She is also using her imagination to supplement the actual happenings.

When you write a column of this type, you must also recall gestures made and tone of voice which someone said something in, and you must describe those to the reader. In this column, the writer recounts chuckles, frowns, smiles, smirks, and gasps.

If you relay dialogue, you must be certain the quotes are comprehensible to the reader, and you must also be sure that you supply sufficient narrative in-between them so that it's clear to the reader who said what, and at what point. You simply cannot lose your reader in quotes where the situation and the sequence of occurrences are unclear. Make the dialogue short and punchy, easy for the reader to grasp.

Each time the speaker changes, start a new paragraph. Further, don't switch tenses. If you're writing in past tense, don't switch to present. Beginning writers sometimes forget to be consistent.

As for punctuation in dialogue, commas and periods go inside the quotation marks. Dialogue punctuation and capitalization can get confusing, though.

Example:

> "Okay, be right back," the waitress said. (Note: there is a comma after "back." And, "the" has a lowercased "t.")

Another dialogue punctuation example:

> "Speaking of waitresses," Mom said, "does it take that long to get us soup?" (Note: complete sentence from "speaking" to "soup," so use a comma after "waitresses" and "said" and lowercase the "d" on "does."

Still another dialogue punctuation example:

> "I'm really getting hungry," I said. "The person in the next booth is champing chips to the beat of the music—dinner à la Muzak." (Note: two complete sentences. One ends with "said," the other with "Muzak." So, "The" of the second sentence begins with a capital "T."

In the dialogue, the personalities of the people involved should shine through. Yes, of course, in a creative column you can fabricate dialogue (and you should if you're trying to achieve comic effect). Also, don't worry about the dialogue being grammatically correct. After all, in conversation, we don't always speak using correct grammar. Be conversational! It's okay to use words like "dunno" for "don't know," as the columnist uses slang to relay conversation.

The situation you write about must be familiar to readers in some way, something they can identify with, or at least imagine happening. There must be underlying logic and truth to what you are saying, even if you are exaggerating the situation to make it more humorous. You want the reader to nod in agreement with your impressions of the situation. If readers don't react to your column emotionally, by laughing, crying, or at least feeling that they've gotten some food for thought, then you haven't made your point, or you've picked a blah topic.

In this particular column, almost anyone can relate to the situation. Practically everyone has been to a restaurant and experienced some of the same things this writer has, on at least a few occasions: tearing open the little plastic mock-cream containers; paying a lot of money for simple fare which has been "gourmetized;" waiting a long time before being served; and receiving someone else's check, among other things. In this column, for comic effect, the writer exaggerates the situation, but the underlying truth is still there. For example, she inflates the food prices, but the truth is, patrons are usually paying very high prices for simple food.

The writer recreates the atmosphere: the Muzak and the rug sweeping, for example. Even if all of these experiences didn't really happen to the writer when she dined with her mother, she's probably experienced all of them in her various restaurant outings throughout the years. She's used her imagination and writing skills to craft them into a column with good sequence. And, she's used descriptive language: similes (such as "pivot like a pulsating statue") and verbs (such as "gushed" and "champing"). Always remember that descriptive language is a part of any column, especially a creative one.

Chapter 4

THE

INFORMATIONAL

COLUMN

(By The Hobbyist Or Professional In The Workplace)

If you are writing an informational column on a topic of your expertise, whether it's on your hobby or your professional skill, you must take great pains not to sound as if you are instructing people in an academic or school-like manner. If you are a professor of economics, switch gears, and get away from sounding as if you are teaching your students. If you are a lawyer, you must not sound as if you are writing a legal document. If you are explaining your hobby of home repair, you must not sound as if you are explaining something from a workbook.

Information can be presented in a non-instructional sounding way. First of all, as usual, you must forget the English composition style of writing the first sentence as a statement of what your column is about. If you are writing a column on stamp collecting, do not, for example, write: "In this column, I'll be discussing how to collect stamps from Africa." Instead, you could begin with, for example, "Collecting stamps from Africa can be a delight with the hodgepodge of colorful animals represented."

As far as the content of the column, don't bore the reader by working up to your points. For example, I've seen attorneys write legal advice columns, starting out by posing a question, then dragging the reader through boring paragraph after boring paragraph, not giving the reader an answer until the final sentence. The journalistic method is to have stated the problem, given the answer, and then supported the answer with subsequent paragraphs of explanation. Never abuse your reader's attention span.

As a columnist, your goal should be not only to inform the public, but to do it in an entertaining manner. This doesn't mean that you have to be a comedian or even a word smith, but you can make an effort to attract the reader's attention and hold it.

Remember that a journalist's writing only comes alive with specific examples. I'm not only talking about specific examples in the body of your column, but I'm also talking about how you can draw your reader into the column by using a basic principle of journalistic writing: begin your column using an example, even if it means fabricating an example or altering it to protect a person. Following is an example of drawing the reader into a column on alcoholism, written by a psychologist. (Note the journalistic technique of using a fictitious name, followed by writing "fictitious name" in parentheses to protect identity, and at the same time to signal this fact to the reader.)

Example:

> Thirty years ago, I knew a man named
> David (fictitious name) who was having

serious financial problems. His business partner had withdrawn a large sum from their bank account without his knowledge, and had invested the money in bonds that proved worthless. Every single cent was lost. David, who was not only on the verge of bankruptcy, had been having serious marital problems for two years, and had just found out his wife was having an affair. He had begun drinking occasionally during his period of marital problems, and eventually his drinking had escalated to where he even had liquor on his breath at 10 a.m.

In the preceding example, you see that this informational column on alcoholism draws the reader into the "story." Assuming that the psychologist's purpose is to instruct others on how to deal with this common problem, rather than start out by talking about a disease, he's giving an example of a person with the disease to "entertain" the reader. As a professional, in order not to defy the principles of confidentiality, you might want to start out by talking about an individual who is facing a certain problem—an individual who is partially or totally fabricated. (I know I told you not to fabricate information, but in this case, it's necessary.)

Whatever you do, if you're writing a column about a problem, don't begin by writing in English composition style, such as in the following: "Today, alcoholism affects (a certain number) of people in the United States."

Another example of drawing the reader into the column is by starting out like this: "John (fictitious name) remembers when he couldn't start out for the office each morning without having his fix of two cans of beer. He would get up before his wife and two school-age children and head for the kitchen in his robe, guzzle down the beers, and then take a shower." Get the idea? Tell an interesting story to illustrate a problem.

Even if you're writing these informational columns on serious topics within your professional expertise, you've got to entertain your reader by grabbing his attention with a situation he can relate to. For example, if you're writing a column on money matters, and you've chosen the topic of credit problems as one of your weekly topics, you might begin your column with a hypothetical example of someone who abused credit card use and went into debt for a lot of money. (Remember, don't use a real-life example because you don't want any libel problems by embarrassing someone and causing their reputation to be damaged. This goes for any topic where social stigma or confidentiality is concerned.)

Example:

> Todd (fictitious name), a young husband and father in his 30s, was on the executive fast-track with a sales management job which paid $60,000 a year. However, with a newly-purchased home of $150,000, two brand new cars, one of which was a Mercedes, and a yacht, he found himself borrowing against his five credit cards.

After you've drawn the reader into your column, be thorough with your facts, in explaining a particular problem.

For example, if you are a psychiatrist who is writing a column about nervousness and tension, after you've given a profile of a person who suffers from it, do not launch into statements like: "Nervousness manifests itself in insomnia, heart palpitations, sweating, and other symptoms." Name as many common symptoms as you can. A complete and comprehensible explanation is essential. You see, in this case, you don't want your readers to confuse nervousness with a disease which could go untreated. As I mentioned previously in this book, do not use technical jargon without explaining in layperson's terms what it means. This is especially hard for medical professionals to remember.

If you're a professional in another area, don't use words or terms which the English language has adopted from other languages like "persona non grata." Also avoid often-unknown foreign words such as in the case of saying: "This trend is 'très' popular." Dropping French words or other foreign words, here and there, which many people can't figure out, is unnecessary. Remember, if you use these words or terms, many of your readers will feel excluded, and you may turn them off to reading this column and your future ones.

Also avoid obscure vocabulary which the average reader may have to look up in a dictionary. Intellectual curiosity is not often a trait of the average reader of general interest publications, such as newspapers. Pedantic vocabulary turns them off. People don't always read to increase their vocabulary.

In addition, columnists who have information to impart are often vague in explaining key points and redundant in their statements. You must avoid these traps, and learn how to write journalistically.

When writing an informational column, be thorough with your facts. After you've written your topic, there shouldn't be any questions in your readers' minds about your topic. At this point, you're probably saying to yourself, "Boy, does this author waste space saying the obvious!" It may be obvious, but it's hard to put into practice unless you've had a lot of experience writing in a step-by-step manner for the "common man." Often, doctors, lawyers, Ph.Ds., and business people assume a certain level of intelligence, knowledge, or even common sense on the part of the average person pertaining to their topic.

While I'm not saying that the average person is stupid, remember that laypeople may not have the foggiest idea of what your topic of expertise is about. Therefore, especially if you are a professional writing an informational column, have a friend who has little or no knowledge of your expertise read over your column to make sure everything is explained thoroughly and clearly. Remember, as a professional who is imparting your knowledge, you should be offering solutions to your readers' problems. But, how can you do this, if they can't understand your advice?

Do not have a colleague or your secretary read over your column. Even your secretary has picked up too much knowledge of your field (and technical jargon) through osmosis.

Along similar lines, don't place yourself above your readers by talking down to them. Be human. Empathize with your readers. For example, if you're writing an investment column, tell your readers of past investment mistakes you've made. Don't think they'll look down on you, but rather, they'll appreciate your candor and learn from your past mistakes.

In an informational column, you can sometimes break down complicated or lengthy information by itemizing your points. For example, instead of taking up two paragraphs stating and later explaining what the safest investments are for someone with $10,000 to invest, you could itemize the safest investments, and afterwards explain each one in detail. Use bullets to itemize.

Example:

- Treasury bills
- Certificates of deposit
- Money markets
- Mutual funds
- Muncipal bonds

Itemizing points also saves a lot of time for the reader who may clip out your column for future reference and later, he'll be able to locate your main information quickly without scanning the entire article again.

When I talk about being thorough with your facts, you might keep in mind that a journalist strives to thoroughly report the "who, what, when, where, whys and hows." If you are, for example, directing readers to where they might seek additional help for a particular problem that you've described, besides naming organizations, also give addresses and phone numbers with area codes. If these organizations are located in the same town as the publication your column runs in, you must still be specific and list the address and phone. Never assume your readers have already heard of the organization. (Besides, there are always newcomers moving into town.) If, however, you are mentioning a social service organization where readers can go to for help, and you must conceal the specific address for purposes of privacy (i.e. halfway houses don't publicize their addresses), then be sure you give the name of a contact person and phone number so that the reader can follow up. Remember, your readers aren't always motivated people, so provide them with as much information as you can. Do everything but make the phone call for them!

A way to remember to be thorough with facts and avoid vagueness, is to put yourself in the reader's shoes. Don't for example, make statements such as "Prudent people should invest in treasury bills and other similar investments." Just what are those "other similar investments?" Along the same lines, do not state: "It is inexpensive to invest in zero coupon bonds." Remember that what is inexpensive to one person, is not to another. Always specify just what the cost is.

Let me give you another example of being as specific as you can be. If you are writing about drug abuse, and you are using a (hypothetical) example of a drug abuser, specifically state what kinds of drugs he's abused. Never make statements such as, "He used cocaine, marijuana, amphetamines, etc." Avoid the use of "etc. " which requires the reader to use his imagination to fill in the blank. (I hope I haven't used an "etc." in this book. It's always a temptation!)

Similarly, don't make statements such as, "He began taking drugs because he was having serious job problems and other problems, too." Remember, it's more interesting to the reader if you give examples of his job and other problems. Was his boss giving him a bad time, criticizing his performance? "Other problems, too" is simply unacceptable. Always give the reader specifics to draw him into your "story."

If you are a social worker, for example, and you are writing a column about how family caretakers can help the elderly, specifically mention certain techniques caretakers can use in helping the elderly to carry out even basic functions, such as help with dressing, bathing, and eating.

Let's talk a little bit more about being thorough with a topic. You may wonder just how you can be thorough, given the fact that you are limited in length in any given column. Yes, it's hard to pick a topic narrow enough to cover in your allotted word space. However, with some topics which have various facets to them, you could discuss one facet of the topic in one column, and inform your reader that in the next two columns, for example, you'll be covering different facets of that topic. For example, if you want to cover alcoholism in detail, you cannot hope to cover all aspects of alcoholism in one column. Therefore, you may want to run a series of columns on the topic. Your first column may be an overview of alcoholism. Your subsequent columns may delve into specific areas such as dealing with the teen-age alcoholic.

If you have a regular informational column running within your field of expertise, but you want to cover a timely topic on one occasion which you are not specifically skilled to speak authoritatively on, you could write this column by interviewing a colleague who can supply you with information and be quoted. Avoid, however, writing a column full of quotes. Instead, paraphrase whenever possible.

Let's take an example. If you are a professional in the field of business, and one week you'd like to write a column about being a small businessman, though you've never been one yourself, you could interview a small home-based businessman who produces and markets a product. You could reveal the rewards of being self-employed, along with the pitfalls and disadvantages. Be thorough and include human interest details, too. Specifically describe how the man creates the product and markets it. Go visit his home-based operation, and report on it firsthand. Obviously, by viewing something firsthand, you can better report on it. How and where is the product created in his home? In his garage? In his basement? Is the product created assembly-line fashion? Do members of his family help him? Get a quote from a family member, too? How does the family member feel about having a business operated out of the home? Does it inconvenience the family? How do they keep work and family life separate?

In keeping with the journalistic "who, what, when, where, whys and hows," ask background questions, such as how it was that he decided to start a home-based business. What was he employed at before? Also ask, when he started the business, why he started it, and how he started it—with loans? Where did he get the loans? Did he start the business on a shoestring budget? How much of his own funds did he use? Ask what the dollar amount of his sales were for the past year. (Presumably, you've picked an interviewee who is financially successful and won't mind publicizing this fact.) Ask what his goals are for the business.

Humanize your "story" by asking the interviewee what he likes and dislikes about being self-employed. Your reader, after all, wants to get an idea of how being self-employed at a home-based business might suit him.

Further, whenever you interview someone, it is often relevant to ask their age. Editors like to see this information. (If you think they're not being truthful about their age, don't include it in your column, however.)

As a columnist, you may be short on time, depending on what your schedule is like and what other responsibilities you juggle. Therefore, if you do set up an interview time, be prepared and go with a list of several key questions to ask (as discussed in the previous chapter.) Only an unprofessional writer expects all his questions to come to him on the spur of the moment. If you go without a well thought-out list, you'll likely forget at least a few of your most important questions. (Note: make sure that the interviewee is clear on the interview time. When you call to schedule the interview, be sure to leave your phone number with the interviewee in case he needs to reach you to reschedule it. You don't, for example, want to drive a long distance only to find that the interviewee had an "emergency." Another word of caution: if you schedule the interview at a distant date, you might call the day before the interview to confirm it, just in case the interviewee has a bad memory or doesn't write appointments down.)

When I was a columnist, I always kept a backlog of column ideas and people to interview, so that if an interview fell through at the last minute, I could quickly proceed with another column idea.

In interviewing someone, always be thinking of giving your reader curious human interest tidbits. In the case of interviewing a self-employed business owner, report on any interesting ironies in his life. Did he, for example, own a previous business, similar to this one, that failed? Why did it fail? If his business has an unusual name, ask the owner why he gave it such a name and report this to your reader. Remember, your readers will wonder about this, if you don't explain it. You will always attract readers and sustain their interest by including curious tidbits, here and there. When you interview someone, be casual in your tone, and pretend you were chatting with a friend. This will put the interviewee more at ease.

In general, pretend you are Johnny Reporter and gather as much information as you can. Don't settle for vague or ambiguous answers from the interviewee. If you are not sure you understand facts or figures he's giving you, stop and ask for a clarification or for an example. Ask "how" or "why," to get him to be more specific with any vague statements he makes. After all, if you don't understand information which an interviewee has given you, how will your reader understand it?

As far as quoting the interviewee, never quote someone if he's blatantly boasting about himself or his business. Maybe in the latter case, to give the reader a somewhat objective idea of the person's business success, you could quote one of his clients, and you should, of course, give your own unbiased opinion. (In the former case, ask the interviewee for the name and phone number of one of his clients.)

If you're interviewing an expert in some area of your field, never quote him extensively in your column, thereby allowing him to take over your whole column with his opinions. Instead, let your opinions dominate the column, supported by the expert's comments.

Let's switch gears a bit. If your hobby is cooking and you're a food columnist, you could also do a column where you're interviewing someone connected with food. Instead of interviewing a restaurateur, why not try something original like interviewing someone who produces a crop like pumpkins? A pumpkin farmer, you ask? Blah, you think. Personally, I don't think so. After all, think of the delicious recipes which can be created by using pumpkins. Incidentally, this would be a good column to get published just prior to Halloween.

In this case, you could fill the reader in on the pumpkin farmer's operation (from firsthand observation, of course), besides including his or his wife's favorite pumpkin recipe. Let's brainstorm and consider possible interview questions leading to the writing of the column. (When I brainstorm before an interview, I don't put questions in any particular order, so they won't be in order, here, either. I don't do encyclopedia research on the topic, either, since I ask basic questions anyone would ask, and that the reader would ask.)

Interview Questions

1) Describe what you see at the farm. Carts of pumpkins? Pumpkins growing on a vine?
2) How many tons of pumpkins does the farmer grow a year?
3) When are the seeds planted?
4) How many seeds are planted per row? (Ask the farmer.)
5) How many rows?
6) How many helpers does he have on the farm? What are the tasks to be done?

7) Are there different kinds of pumpkins? Describe the different kinds and does this farmer grow all kinds?

8) What is the farmer's busiest and slowest time of year?

9) What is the average size of a pumpkin and how long does it take to grow?

10) Where do the pumpkins go after they leave his farm?

11) Are the pumpkins a more profitable or less profitable crop than other vegetables? Ask the farmer to give specific comparisons.

12) How are pumpkins nutritious? What vitamins do they contain?

13) Are the pumpkins high in calories? How high? (The farmer's wife would probably know this. If not, you could look this information up.)

14) Where are pumpkins commonly grown in this country?

15) Where are pumpkins commonly grown in other parts of the world? (Ask the farmer, don't do research on this.)

16) In what climates do pumpkins grow best and why?

17) When did the farmer start his business? If it's a family business, when did he inherit the business, and how long has it been in the family?

18) Age of the farmer?

19) Describe the farmer in physique, if you think it's relevant.

20) What does he like about being a pumpkin farmer?

21) What doesn't he like about farming pumpkins?

22) Does the farmer invite local school children to come out for a trip to his farm?

23) Does the farmer know how the children's custom of carving pumpkins as jack-o-lanterns came about and when?

24) Does his wife bake a lot of pumpkin pies? How many a year?

25) What else do they make with pumpkins?

26) Include their favorite family pumpkin pie recipe or one of their other pumpkin recipes at the end of your column.

Remember, not all the answers the farmer gives you to these questions will be interesting enough to work into your column. Include only the most interesting information in your column. (Besides, you won't have room to include everything, depending on your space limitations.) Don't give your reader a complete course in pumpkins. My point in brainstorming for a lot of interview questions is to let you become aware of all the possibilities in writing this type of column. How much does the average person who loves to cook really know about pumpkins, even though he may use them in cooking? It is interesting, for example, to educate your reader on how nutritious pumpkins are, and how high in calories they are. But, remember to entertain your reader with facts about the farmer's business, while you're at it.

Other Tips On Writing Informational Columns

When providing your reader with information, make it as easy to grasp as possible. For example, if you're a health professional writing about a disease, instead of saying that 90,000 Americans suffer from a certain disease, break down the information in such a way that the reader can relate to it. Example: One in every (X number) of Americans suffers from (such and such a disease).

Remember, always include interesting and relevant tidbits of information or ironies. For example, in interviewing the pumpkin farmer, did you find that he once lived in the city and that he traded in his "business suit job" for the "country blue jean life?"

Further, don't bring up a new or related topic in the body of your column without discussing it adequately. Beginning writers often frustrate readers by bringing up a new topic and then stating, "But that's another column in itself, so I won't go into it." What does this accomplish except to leave your reader hungering for more information?

As a practical point, besides checking the spelling of people's names, check the spelling of names of businesses and organizations you are writing about. Remember, business names often deviate in spelling from the way they would commonly be spelled. Besides the fact that misspellings lead to complaints from the public, remember that you'll also lose credibility with editors and the interviewee. In the latter case, he may not want to be interviewed in the future.

Sample Column

Let's look at a sample informational column below. In the following fabricated column, there are typical mistakes made by beginning non-journalistic writers. While reading the column, make notes to yourself about what is lacking in content and style. Be sure to number the paragraphs, so you can follow the commentary, afterwards.

This is the column:

Problems with Jimmy or Suzie misbehaving? Although misbehavior is common in all children while they are growing up, this fact in itself, doesn't make it any less frustrating for parents. And often, parents don't know how to handle and remedy the problem.

If you want to help your Suzie to stop misbehaving, you must discover why she is misbehaving and treat the cause, instead of the symptom or actual misbehavior. You must be like a physician who sees that Mr. Frink, his patient, has a nervous twitch, so he attempts to discover if there is a physical cause behind it, so that he can treat the cause.

When one behaves in a certain way, one is expressing inner feelings. A child, for example, may have a particular inner need and may exhibit a certain behavior if he feels that the behavior will fulfill the need. For example, a child who wants attention might resort to crying in order to get it.

Misbehavior can take on unusual twists. For example, misbehavior at home is not always a symptom of a problem at home. Instead, it may be a symptom of a school problem. If a child is unhappy at school and doesn't get along with his teacher, he may become uncooperative when his parents ask him to do something.

As a parent, if you deal with the uncooperative behavior at home, you may end up eliminating that behavior when it occurs around you. However, if the child is still feeling uncomfortable at school, he'll continue to have school problems. Therefore, misbehavior will sometimes take some investigative work on your part. (Put on your Sherlock Holmes' hat.)

Children commonly misbehave by rebelling, fighting, lying, or stealing. These forms of misbehavior signal the child's basic needs: the need to be able to control his environment, for example. Some misbehaviors occur when a child is not allowed to take responsibility for his own actions.

There are a few things parents should keep in mind when dealing with misbehavior: (1) There is a cause for all misbehavior; (2) Misbehavior is only a symptom of that cause; (3) The cause behind acts of misbehavior must be discovered before the misbehavior can be stopped.

The parent who takes the time to understand his child and discover what his feelings are, will find it easier to discover the causes of his misbehavior.

The important point to remember in dealing with misbehavior is that your child is not a bad one, even though his behavior is bad. In your mind, try to separate the child from the behavior. This is hard for parents and sometimes even for teachers to do, but you must strive to.

You must properly guide your child. Don't ignore him or his behavior problem. Even if you have a demanding job or schedule, don't ignore your child when you are home. Quality time, not necessarily quantity time, is the key. Above all, don't make excuses for your child's behavior. For example, don't let the teacher be the scapegoat. Focus on the child and work toward correcting the problem with him.

Commentary

In this column, the content is not only lacking, but the structure of the piece is completely reversed. Significant points are not made until the end, instead of being brought up in the beginning.

What troubles us the most, is that if this column was supposed to teach us about misbehavior, then why didn't it include ways to deal with misbehavior, too? After all, it doesn't help one to know that you should seek to identify causes for the misbehavior if one doesn't also know how to handle the misbehavior once its cause has been identified. This column doesn't serve the reader in a practical way, in that it doesn't give him a solution to how to actually deal with misbehavior. Why give your reader only the first steps to the solution?

Once you identify the cause of the misbehavior, then what? Suppose your kid is misbehaving because he doesn't like his teacher. Once you identify that, what do you do? How do you deal with the teacher? Or, suppose your kid has become a brat because the other kids in school are teasing him. What do you do about this?

Let's look at the column closely.

Paragraph 1. This is a good lead paragraph. We are introduced to the topic in a fairly interesting way. (Unfortunately, as we later see, the columnist never ends up discussing all that he leads us to believe he will, including how to remedy the problem.)

Paragraph 2. This is also a good paragraph as it introduces you to the first step you must take in dealing with misbehavior: identification of the cause before treatment begins. Further, the writer gives you the analogy about the physician to clarify his point. Remember, in writing a journalistic piece, it is good to use analogies to bring home a point.

Paragraph 3. This paragraph is fine, but it could have been preceded by paragraphs 8, 9, and 10, in this order, instead of saving these three key paragraphs until the end. Remember, don't build up to main points. Also, in paragraph 3, the writer should have given a few more examples of "particular inner needs" and the behavior that a child uses to get them.

Paragraph 4. In this paragraph, the writer could have used one more example of misbehavior with an "unusual twist."

Paragraph 5. This paragraph is confusing and incomplete. Just what should a parent do to eliminate misbehavior at home? And, what should the parent do about the school problem, once it has been identified, so the misbehavior doesn't continue there?

Paragraph 6. The first two sentences of this paragraph should have come much earlier in the column. For example, they could have been inserted as the last two sentences of paragraph 1. Further, "the need to be able to control his environment" is vague and sounds like professional jargon. This could be simply put: "the need to be in control." As for the last sentence of paragraph 6, it is unclear. We need examples of what the columnist is talking about when he says "when the child is not allowed to take responsibility for his own actions."

Paragraph 7. This paragraph is redundant and therefore, should be omitted. (It could have been included in the first few paragraphs of the piece.) Always remember not to summarize points at the end of your piece which you should have summarized at the beginning.

In this column, in general, besides not telling us how to deal with misbehavior, the columnist omits other essential information. One wonders, for example, if by merely asking a child about what's bothering him, if that leads to identifying the cause of the misbehavior. After all, sometimes a child doesn't want to tell you what's bothering him. Then what? Further, what about very small children who misbehave? For example, how do you handle a three-year-old's misbehavior? Isn't a three-year-old, for example, often unable to tell you what's bothering him? Therefore, how does one go about identifying the cause of misbehavior in younger children?

All in all, it is a columnist's duty to develop a topic as fully as possible. Unfortunately, this columnist appears not to have even tried.

Another Column To Analyze

Let's look at another fabricated column (with fictitious names and facts). This column has many of the same problems as the previous one. Read the following column, makes notes on the problems you see with it. Lastly, number the paragraphs before reading the commentary which follows it.

This is the column:

Do you think you might be interested in further pursuing your hobby of gardening and broadening your horticultural knowledge? Spring really isn't so far off, and now is the time to resurrect your green thumb. You don't have to be a professional horticulturist to do a professional maintenance job on your property and to allow your garden to radiate with color. Picture in your mind a wonderland of budding flowers.

Zigland County Extension Office will offer its Expert Home Gardener Program for the very first time in its history. Horticulturists, myself included, are seeking participants 21 and older. We've designed a program to offer a variety of educational opportunities to interested home gardeners.

Participants will receive 30 hours of free training by professional horticulturists, during five sessions, in various horticultural areas of possible interest to the hobbyist. Participants will be working with a variety of plants and trees. Classes will meet at the county extension office complex in Hartland and will consist of both classroom training and slide presentations and practical hands-on individual instruction. All tools will be provided, but participants should bring a pair of gloves and should wear comfortable clothing. They should also bring a sack lunch. Beverages will be provided.

In exchange for their training, certified Expert Home Gardeners will be expected to volunteer 40 hours of service to help answer gardening questions phoned in to the extension office during the hectic growing season or to help with various other programs during the year.

One of the Expert Home Gardener training periods will be held Thursdays during the day beginning February 11 and ending March 12. Session Two will be held on Saturdays beginning February 13 and ending March 14.

If you are interested in discovering more about this program, you may contact the county extension office at 761-7000. After receiving completed applications, we will be selecting participants for each session by Feb. 5.

If there is sufficient interest in the Expert Home Gardener program, it will continue on a regular basis and be expanded to include more participants.

Commentary

Many local informational columnists use their columns from time to time to update the community on programs of interest to them. This is acceptable, as long as the column doesn't sound like merely a short press release— a notice with a few facts about an event, its time, date and place. This column is not well-developed in content, and it does read more like a press release. It doesn't provide much specific information and is blah sounding. It is merely a notice to get interested people to phone in for information.

This columnist could have provided much more detailed information, and made the column more interesting, thereby attracting more participants to call in and get interested in the program.

Let's look at how this column is lacking in information, and let's also consider how it could have been written in journalistic style.

Paragraph 1. This paragraph is acceptable as far as content. However, it is too wordy, and therefore an editor would consider it to be cumbersome to read. Journalists, especially columnists, make every effort to economize on words. Columnists, in particular, are usually asked to limit their word count. All journalists can strive to limit their word count with factual statements. As for another flaw in this paragraph, this columnist could have stated things in a lighter, livelier way. For example, he could have said, "Interested in pursuing your gardening hobby and broadening your horticultural knowledge? Spring isn't far off, so green thumbs up! No need to be a professional to maintain your property and allow your garden to radiate with color." (Note: in the former sentence, I've omitted the word "horticulturist" which is implied. And, don't repeat the word "professional" for the second time as in "professional maintenance job." Simply say, "to maintain your property.")

Paragraph 2. This paragraph is redundant and vague. In the first sentence, all that needs to be said is: "Zigland County Extension Office is offering a new program, Expert Home Gardener." This cuts the number of words. In the last sentence, instead of saying "a variety of educational opportunities," the columnist should have specified what they are. One other note: instead of waiting until Paragraph 5 to tell us when the new program will be offered, this information should be given here. Otherwise, the reader keeps asking himself: "When is it?" In paragraph 2, the columnist could even just state that the program will begin in February (for brevity), and leave the specific dates until paragraph 5.

Paragraph 3. Here again, the content is vague and redundant. What are the "various horticultural areas of possible interest to the hobbyist?" What kinds of plants and trees will be involved? We wonder, too, what the slide presentations will be on and how much classroom time will be involved, in compared to practical work. Further, what practical hands-on instruction will be included? As for redundancy, in the first sentence, to say "professional horticulturists" is unnecessary. "Horticulturists" will do. In fact, we already learned in paragraph 2 who would be teaching the class. As for the last two sentences (about tools, clothing, food, and beverages), this information could have been saved until the end of the column since these facts aren't crucial. (Note: as for common journalistic style, lowercase "county extension office" when the proper name "Zigland" does not precede it.)

Paragraph 4. As for content, this paragraph is also vague. What specific months does the hectic growing season involve? And what specific "help with various other programs during the year" are needed? For what programs?

Paragraph 5. As for style, the first sentence should

read: "One training period will be (state specific times), Thursdays, Feb. 11 to March 12." ("During the day" is vague. Is it from 10 a.m. to 4 p.m.?) The second sentence should read "Session Two will be held from 10 a.m. to 4 p.m., Saturdays, Feb. 13 to March 14." (Abbreviate months. Also note the way I have cut verbiage in this rewritten version.)

Paragraph 6. The content is vague. One wonders what criteria will be used to select participants. Is it by level of experience? This is important. Readers wonder, at this point, if they should even bother to pick up the telephone to further investigate the program. Further, the first sentence of this paragraph should be the last sentence of the column. Always leave the phone number to call until the last sentence. (In addition, instead of saying, "If you are interested in knowing more about this program, you may contact...," simply state: "Those interested in knowing more, may contact ..." Always economize on words.

Paragraph 7. As for content, we wonder when the program is anticipated to continue, so that readers who may not be able to attend in February can plan for a possible different time.

Concluding words: although including all these specifics may strike you as nitpicking, editors look for them.

Additional Note

In general, besides writing informational columns based on news about programs available to the public in your professional or hobbyist field, you can also consider writing question and answer columns for imparting information. However, if you don't have an arrangement with your editor to write a question and answer column all the time, you should ask your editor how he feels about including one periodically. Some editors don't like question and answer columns, particularly if you are a columnist for a local publication, because they feel that they can easily pick up a column by a nationally-syndicated columnist in the question and answer format. Some editors may feel that the question and answer format is a copout for a local columnist who won't have to go to the trouble of writing and organizing a whole column. These editors prefer that a local columnist take the time and energy to delve into a single topic and discuss it at length.

Personally, I feel that if you write an informational column, you can legitimately run a question and answer column periodically if you feel that the readers' questions which are sent to you by mail are piling up. However, with question and answer columns, be selective. Pick only those questions sent to you by readers which would benefit the majority of your readership. Don't waste space in your column by answering obscure questions which only a minority of your readership would possibly be interested in learning about.

As far as answering questions which readers write in about, remember that readers may pose them in a vague way. Therefore, for the benefit of your readership, edit them for clarity and conciseness. (Important: don't identify the reader by name—use initials—especially if it's a question of a personal nature. In this case, assume the reader does not want to be identified.)

In answering questions, don't talk down to the reader by saying something like, "You don't seem to understand that..." (I once saw a lawyer-columnist do this in his question and answer column.) There is simply no reason to belittle your reader. And, the tone of this lawyer seems to translate into: "You are bothering me with foolishness!"

Besides including a question and answer column from time to time, you may also want to make mention of a new book pertinent to your field, written by a colleague or some authority. Unless you are a book review columnist, you don't need to spend your entire column space discussing a new book. You could, instead, make mention of it in the last paragraph of your column, if the book's topic relates to this particular column. However, if you feel this new book is unique and worthy of being reviewed in full in your column because the subject is timely, do so, but don't merely regurgitate the information in the book. Give your comments and opinions on the topic and call the author up for a quote to draw the reader into your column. Tell your reader: "In a recent telephone interview with me, the author made the comment that ..." The author's quote could elaborate on an important point that the book touched on. Remember, whenever you are writing an informational column, give your reader something that he cannot get elsewhere. In the case of a book review, it's important not to just summarize the book, but to get the reader interested in reading it.

Further, if the book is published by an obscure publisher, it may not be available in all bookstores. Therefore, in this case, give the address of the publisher and the cost of the book (plus shipping charge) so your readers can readily obtain it.

Additional note: as a columnist, authors, publishers, and publicists will often send you new books to mention or review in your column. This is fine, and if unsolicited, don't feel obligated to review them. If you review books from time to time, don't be tempted to request free review copies from publishers which you don't plan to review—to use them as gifts or whatever. You are a professional writer, and keep this in mind at all times. Don't exploit your position in this way. And yes, if you're also an author, toot your horn and make mention of your new book that has just come out.

One More Column To Analyze

The following fabricated column, with information gleaned from a variety of student papers, is another example of a flawed column. By now, you're probably good at picking out problems with content and style. Do as you've done before: read the column and take notes. Then, number the paragraphs (all indentations) before reading the commentary.

This is the column:

Thinking of choosing a wine for your next dinner party, but you don't know how to select one?

Don't feel embarrassed, because most people don't. Many people get confused when they walk into their local wine shop or drift over to the supermarket wine section. They are bombarded with rows of attractive bottles of all shapes, colors, and sizes which have labels with designs of beautiful vineyards.

Labels are useful in selecting a good bottle of wine, and I'll give you a brief lesson in what label information means.

Let's take the vintage year. You should know that the vintage year posted on a wine bottle is not totally accurate. It is, in fact, only 95 percent accurate since 95 percent of the grapes are harvested and crushed in that year.

As for the words, "produced and bottled by," this means that the bottler has made at least 75 percent of the wine from the crushing of the grapes. This does not necessarily mean, however, that the vintner has grown the grapes.

And, what does "estate bottled" mean? This means that the grapes come from just one vineyard. However, this can mean grapes from a variety of locations because large vintners have scattered land holdings.

When a certain area is designated on a label, this is helpful, too. To be labeled "California," for example, the grapes must be grown in the state.

Another thing which people wonder about is which vintners can be counted on to produce good wines. My favorite ones are: Charles Krug, Wente Bros., and Sutter Home. And, when a good wine maker labels a bottle "private reserve," this is worth paying attention to because it is a sign of its being considered special.

Perhaps the most commonly-asked question is, "How

do you interpret the alcohol percentage of a wine?" Answer: Light alcoholic wines may contain as little as eight percent alcohol. Ten percent also constitutes a wine of light alcoholic content. German white wines also contain the latter percentage. Ten to 14 percent is typical for American table wines. Fourteen percent alcoholic content is a fairly alcoholic wine. Claret, a still wine from France with a rich ruby color, is an example.

Fortified wines are those in which spirits such as brandy, are added to increase the strength or alcoholic content. For example, sherry is one of the fortified wines and it contains 18 to 21 percent alcohol. French and Italian vermouth are fortified wines to which aromatic herbs and spices have been added. These are called aromatized wines.

When you've bought a bottle of wine, but don't plan to use it for a long time, how do you store it? Upright? On its side?

An upright bottle causes the cork to dry out and the air to seep in. Air is not good for wine, so tightly-corked bottles are needed to preserve a wine's bouquet and flavor. If wine is stored on its side, the wet cork will keep out the air. However, this is important only for the more expensive wines. For cheaper wines, it usually doesn't matter since most people often consume them right after purchasing them.

I once bought a low-priced clear white wine and left it on my shelf for two years. When I finally opened it, I found that sediment had accumulated. And when I tasted it, blah! There was absolutely no flavor left. So, the moral of this story is: use lower-priced wines soon after purchase. Sediment should not be allowed to accumulate in clear wines.

Should you give your wine a chance to "breathe"? This is debatable. According to some experts, wines should be opened early so they can breathe before serving. However, other experts think this doesn't make much difference, and they don't go to the trouble of doing it.

What about leftover wine from your dinner party? It is best to store leftover wine in a full bottle. Got an old pop bottle? If so, fill it to the top with wine, seal it tightly, and store it in the refrigerator. This way, the wine should keep for about a week.

Keeping these points in mind, you should have an easier time selecting and serving wine on your next special occasion. As the Italians say, salute e buon appetito!

Commentary

In general, this column is very confusing in content and does not accomplish what the writer set out to do, as stated in his lead sentence. The column doesn't aid the reader in selecting a wine for a dinner party. It merely gives him bits of vague and unrelated information and statistics which he doesn't really need. There are no smooth transitions between these paragraphs, either. If the reader is to be able to select a wine for his next dinner party, the columnist should have, for example, presented him with examples of what wines go well with what types of food or particular dishes.

Let's look at the details.

Paragraphs 1 & 2. These paragraphs are fine in that they will attract many readers who often read wine columns and even those who don't usually read them. Incidentally, a one-sentence paragraph—Paragraph 1—is fine, and is often used by journalists.

Paragraph 3. This demonstrates bad column style. A reader shouldn't be told that he's getting "a brief lesson." This sounds as if he'll be going to school. It would have been better to state, "Labels are useful in selecting a good bottle of wine, only if you know how to interpret them, so let's look at them closely."

Paragraph 4. One wonders about the other five percent of the grapes. When are they harvested and crushed? Besides, is it really necessary to know that the vintage year which is posted is only 95 percent accurate? Doesn't this sound like trivia? And, who dictates this law that 95 percent of the grapes should be harvested and crushed in the vintage year that is posted? Further, specifically how is it determined which vintage years are good? Who determines this? Without giving us examples of which vintage years are good for particular wines, how are we to select a good wine? From the information given, we cannot select a good bottle of wine, and worse, we are given vague information which raises more questions than it answers.

Paragraphs 5 & 6. We are given more vague information which raises more questions than it answers. In paragraph 5, I am confused between the roles of the bottler and the vintner. And, in paragraph 6, couldn't the columnist, for the sake of clarity, have left out the sentence about "grapes from just one vineyard?" (Sentences 2 and 3 of paragraph 6 seem to contradict themselves.)

Paragraph 7. This paragraph supplies us with information which the layperson would consider obvious, so it doesn't need to be included in the column.

Paragraph 8. This information should have come much earlier in the piece. Paragraph 8 should have been paragraph 4. Even though this paragraph gives us some information about wine selection, it is vague and incomplete. The columnist should have told us why these vintners are his favorite, and what particular kinds of wines each excels in. I'd like to find out what makes a good wine. What role does taste play in a good wine? The columnist should specify just what a good wine is. Further, the last sentence of this paragraph is vague. Does private reserve actually mean this wine is better and in what way?

Paragraphs 9 & 10. The information here is interesting and should not have been buried so far down in the column. Although I doubt that most people choose their wine on the basis of its alcoholic content, it would be somewhat interesting to find out how much a few percentage points make a difference in the potency of the wine. The information in these two paragraphs could have been introduced beginning with the fifth paragraph. In paragraph 9, specific examples of wines should have been given. What kinds of wines contain eight percent? Could the columnist suggest good wines in the ten to 14 percent alcohol range? Also, what does a "still" wine mean? And, if the columnist had given specific examples of wines, he could have also told us what type of foods go well with them. I'd also like to know if the taste of wines with eight percent alcohol differ greatly from the ones with 14 percent alcohol? If so, how? Further, couldn't the columnist have told us, broadly speaking, how percentage points make a difference in how quickly one becomes inebriated? For example, is one likely to become drunk after two drinks with 14 percent alcohol, but unlikely to become drunk after two drinks with 10 percent alcohol? As for paragraph 10, when and with what should sherry and vermouth be served with. If they are served, what wines served during the entree would compliment them? For example, if one is serving sherry after the meal, should one choose only an 8 percent alcohol wine to be served during the entree, and what type of wine should that be?

Paragraphs 11, 12 & 13. Actually, paragraphs 14 and 15 should have preceded these paragraphs, because they deal with the dinner party. As for analyzing paragraphs 11, 12, and 13, paragraph 11 is fine.

In paragraph 12, one wonders what the columnist considers to be an expensive wine, as opposed to a cheap wine. Remember that journalists are careful to be specific. After all, what is expensive to one person, isn't necessarily to another. In paragraph 13, one wonders what the columnist considers to be a "low-priced" wine. One also wonders in what wines sediment is acceptable.

Paragraph 14. First, the word "breathe" should not be in quotes, since it isn't an unusual word or a word being used in an unusual way. Second, this paragraph is redundant. It's sufficient to say, "This is debatable, as experts disagree." Third, what's missing in this paragraph is the columnist's opinion. After all, doesn't he think he's an expert and that his opinion counts? If not, he shouldn't be a columnist.

Paragraph 15. This paragraph is fine.

Paragraph 16. This final paragraph only reminds us that the columnist didn't do what he said he was going to do. In a column of this kind, the columnist could have ended by suggesting some wines for your next dinner party, given the particular season of the year, for example. Or, if he was a local columnist, he could have even mentioned news about an upcoming wine event in town. To do this, he could have created a smooth transition by saying something like, "You can get more ideas for serving wine at your dinner party by attending the upcoming wine festival at 2 p.m., Friday, March 30, at the Civic Center." Or, as a final paragraph, the columnist could have mentioned a new wine book out on the market which would offer further suggestions for serving wine at a dinner party. As a final note, the Italian words salute and buon appetito are fine to use, as long as they are spelled correctly. (Here, they are.) Since readers can probably figure out what they mean, in this case, it isn't inappropriate or snobbish to include these foreign words.

Summary Of Key Points

In summarizing some of the things we've been discussing, first of all, always make your lead sentence as snappy as possible, even in an informational column.

Examples of acceptable lead sentences for the wine column which we just analyzed are:

- When you purchase wine, is your decision based merely on a pretty bottle?
- When you purchase wine, do you judge it by its pretty color?
- A pretty label does not a good bottle of wine make.
- What's in a name? Plenty, when it comes to a bottle of wine.

The point is, you should play around with your lead sentence and come up with something bright. Yes, writing your lead sentence is one of the hardest things to do when writing your informational column, because you naturally tend to think in terms of getting your information across without entertaining the reader.

After you write the lead sentence, don't bombard the reader with paragraphs of facts, figures, and percentages in a blow-by-blow fashion as in the wine column. Ask yourself if the reader really wants and needs to hear difficult and technical information. Focus instead, on interesting, less technical information and give it to the reader early in the piece. If you don't know what information would most appeal to the average reader and should therefore be placed early in your column, ask a layperson to read your column. Ask him if the way you presented your information and prioritized your facts was done in the most interesting way. Remember: never build up to the most important information since your reader's attention span is limited and he may not wait until the good stuff comes, if you leave it until late in the piece.

As for the ending, in an informational column, you don't need to end with a bang. You can even taper off with a suggestion of some kind to lead your reader to more information or you can summarize the topic.

As for objectivity in the informational column, if you recommend a product in your column, such as a bottle of wine from a certain vintner, be sure not to do so because you've been paid to endorse it. A columnist must be objective and not be offering advice that he was influenced to give.

Another vital point about objectivity is that an editor will drop you like the handle of a boiling pot if you promote your services right in your column. You are supposed to be informing your reader about a topic, giving him your insights—not running an advertisement about your services. Let your credit line mention who you are and your readers will find you. For example, if you are an attorney, your credit line could read: John Jones is an attorney with the firm of Black, Smith, and White in San Jose.

The Opinion Column On The Op-Ed Page

The Op-Ed pages of a newspaper are its "Opinion-Editorial pages." Besides editor's editorials, there is room for staff writers, syndicated columnists, and/or guest columnists to express their views on issues. The opinion page is often referred to as "opposite the editorial page" so that's why editors also refer to it as "Op-Ed."

I'm including mention of the op-ed piece under this chapter heading of Informational Columns because you can't write such a piece without integrating timely information into it. For example, if you wrote an opinion piece for your local metropolitan newspaper on what you feel is unfair property taxation in your county, then you would obviously have to have done your research on property taxation. You would have had to have read news articles written on the topic, besides giving your opinion and querying individual property owners for an overview of the situation. Opinions on current issues simply cannot be formed without doing your research at the library. In writing an op-ed piece, your writing must encourage thought, raise people's consciousness, or rekindle public awareness on the topic.

Let's take another example for an op-ed piece. Say you would like to write a local piece on how crime in your community has gotten out of hand, and how you feel the solution is to use more of the police budget on community policing to reduce criminal activity. Your piece must be forceful and riveting in tone. You could draw your reader into your column with a narrative, based on your reading of current news articles on the subject: "Last week a paraplegic was brutally bludgeoned in the southwest area of town while three people looked on." In the body of your piece, you should mention relevant statistics on crime and what part of the police budget which is currently being used for other purposes could be diverted to pay for additional community policing—among other elements. Your ending paragraph or sentence should specifically state what action you'd like your readers to take, that is, how they should voice their frustration in order to get matters changed.

In op-ed pieces, controversial topics are relished by editors. What is definitely not welcomed in op-ed pieces are criticisms of large groups such as ethnics, legitimate religious groups, or any other class of people. In addition, although this seems obvious, leave out obscenity and name-calling. (Don't laugh about this. I once read an opinion piece in a community paper in which local teen-age rabble rousers were called "crud." I would guess—in fact, hope—that the editor of the publication missed this before it went into print. The columnist could have picked a better word.)

As a writer, any kind of writer, you must never have an axe to grind. Don't write op-ed pieces to get back at someone or a group of people you're mad at.

In addition, in writing op-ed pieces, it's also important to bring to light an issue by drawing analogies. Let's take the issue of drug paraphernalia being sold in some record shops. I once wrote an op-ed piece about this issue when I was a staffer on a newspaper, because local parents of teenagers were upset about record store merchants doing this. They felt that this sent a message to kids that drugs were socially acceptable. My main point was that I didn't feel that the sale of drug paraphernalia encouraged use of drugs by those kids who frequented the record store just to buy records. After all, an analogy would be that the sale of cocktail glasses in a department store doesn't influence people to use alcohol nor to become alcoholics.

Writing op-ed pieces is a particularly good opportunity if you're an author who's written a book on a timely issue and you want to spin-off an op-ed piece about it. The op-ed piece, of course, would be a good publicity ploy to plug your book. (Don't plug your book in the piece, however. Save the plug for your credit line at the end of the piece.)

In submitting an op-ed piece, never waste time querying the editor as to whether he's interested in the topic. In large metropolitan daily newspapers, just send the manuscript to the editorial page editor. At a small paper, address it in the editor's or managing editor's name. Op-ed pieces are so timely that by the time an editor would get around to responding to your query, your issue may no longer be of interest to the public.

It's good to submit a "head" (title) with your op-ed piece, although it will be adjusted or changed to meet space requirements. The head should be snappy to hook the editor's attention.

Don't feel that you must limit your op-ed piece to newspapers in your region of the country. Large, nationally-circulated metropolitan papers welcome opinion pieces from writers outside their area, if the issue is of national interest, of course. Try these, for example: the *Boston Globe*, *The New York Times*, the *Cleveland Plain Dealer*, the *Detroit Free Press*, the *San Francisco Examiner*, the *Wall Street Journal*, the *Dallas Morning News*, the *Baltimore Evening Sun*, the *Los Angeles Times*, and the *St. Louis Post-Dispatch*. (Read the last chapter of this book for more submission suggestions.)

You know how a lot of writers of op-ed pieces got their feet wet? By writing short letters to the editor of local and national publications, just to build their self-confidence. I, personally, wouldn't consider letters to editors as publishing credits, but the point is, they build your self-esteem and let you know that you can see your name in print on the op-ed pages—that your ideas are valuable.

Chapter 5

STYLE DETAILS

In this chapter, through a variety of exercises and examples, we will deal with how to avoid writing style gaffes, how to economize on words, and how to refine your style. Mastering these concepts will allow you to present yourself to editors as a professional writer.

Part 1. Avoiding Style Gaffes

Whether writing an informational or creative type of column, many beginning columnists fall into some bad style traps. Remember that readers will miss your point if you distract them with poor writing style.

Above all, you should always avoid ranting and raving to make a point.

Do not, for example, do this: "Boy, I hate airplane travel. Really I do. I hate the hassle of deciphering all the super saver fares, purchasing a ticket, and waiting in line to get baggage checked in. I hate the rationing of mock cheese spread, peanuts, and soft drinks on the flight."

Instead of ranting and raving, you could, for example, take the lighthearted approach: "Oh, the challenge of airplane travel. Do you have a Ph.D. to decipher all those super saver fares? Got a novel to read while you're waiting in line to get your baggage checked in? What about in-flight?

While I realize that everyone is weight- conscious these days, the rationing of mock cheese spread, peanuts, and soft drinks isn't a very hospitable way to treat the passengers." Realize that as long as you are making legitimate points, you don't need to directly express your annoyance, hitting the reader over the head with your frustration. Humor, for example, allows the reader to pick up your frustration, and it entertains him, besides.

Another acceptable example, without humor, would be: "Air travel has become a major irritant: the hassle of purchasing a ticket which includes deciphering all the saver fares. Maybe it's just better to 'wing it' without purchasing an advance fare and forget trying to save a few bucks. Then, there's the vigil of waiting in line to get luggage checked in—luggage which usually doesn't arrive until two days later, anyway. In-flight, it doesn't get much better: the mock cheese spread and the rationing of peanuts and soft drinks."

Let's go back to the original "ranting and raving example" to make another point about bad writing. In that example, the writer hops from what happens before take-off to what happens in-flight (the rationing of mock cheese spread) without a transition. The reader isn't led in a systematic thought pattern, but is lost. A smooth transition would have been, "I hate the hassle of deciphering all the super saver fares, purchasing a ticket, and waiting in line to get baggage checked in. In-flight, I hate the rationing of mock cheese spread…" You see, you need the word "In-flight" at the beginning of that sentence to signal the change from being on the ground to being in-flight, so the reader doesn't get confused with your switching gears all of a sudden.

Let's take a closer look at good style which involves smooth transitions. They are particularly important when introducing direct quotes.

Example:

> John Javits of Oak Brook is one who agrees with the proposed taxation changes.
> "I agree with the proposed taxation

> changes, because under this new system all taxpayers would share equally in the burden," he said.
>
> However, others such as Jim Bjorklund of Palatine disagree. "This proposed system doesn't seem right to me," he said.

Compare the previous paragraphs with the bad example which follows:

> John Javits of Oak Brook is one who agrees with the proposed taxation changes. "I agree with the proposed taxation changes, because under this new system all taxpayers would share equally in the burden," he said.
>
> "This proposed system doesn't seem right to me," said Jim Bjorklund of Palatine.

You notice the difference in this bad example. We are hit with the second quote without an introduction that there will be a change in viewpoint from another person.

Besides using smooth transitions, your writing will be easier to read and more organized for the reader to drift through (rather than wade through) if you separate a series of points you are making. This, of course, is especially good to do in an informational column, and it is a sign of a professional journalist. In this case, bullets are often useful to itemize at least three points. If you are writing a medical advice column, for example, you could itemize the symptoms of a disease. Or, if you are writing a business column and you want to state that there are four principles which underlie success in sales, you can summarize and emphasize these points by using bullets.

• Make personal contact with the prospective buyer
• Understand the prospective buyer's needs
• Make follow-up calls to the prospective buyer
• Never try to oversell the prospective buyer

Through this method of itemizing points, it's much easier for the reader to grasp the information, and it allows him to keep these points in mind. It also makes it easier for the reader to refer back to these points, if he needs to, without searching for a particular paragraph which contains these points. Then, after you've summarized these four principles, elaborate on each one, one by one. Whatever you do, never tell the reader that there are four principles (without identifying them at that point) only to state the first and go into a long description of it, state the second and go into a long description of it, (and so on). In other words, don't make the reader have to skip ahead to find out what each principle is, one by one.

Another point about good organization: avoid beating around the bush in a paragraph. Take this example:

> "I'm not sure what's worse about air travel: the purchasing of the ticket or the actual flight. Well... yes I am sure. It's the purchasing of the ticket and trying to sort through all the super saver fares." (In this example, it sounds as if the writer is trying to tease the reader, but for no intelligent purpose.)

Building to false climaxes is just as bad. Example:

> How much did she win in the lottery? Not one million... Not two million... Not four million... But... six million!

In the latter case, there is simply no need to attempt to keep the reader in suspense. If you write in this fashion, your reader will be reminded of a television game show host who teases his audience.

In general, don't impose on your readers' patience or attention span by being vague. Consider this example: He had been a teacher, among other careers.

What are these other careers? Chances are, he didn't have that many careers, making it impractical to mention them all. As another example, avoid usage of "for many years." How many years?

Further, never include terms in your column that you

yourself do not know the meaning of. As an example, let's say you're writing about having gone to a Shirley MacLaine appearance, and you mention that she spoke on a variety of topics including "channeling." Do you know precisely what channeling is? Don't expect your reader to know what it means, if you don't know. If you don't know and can't find out, don't bring the term up in your writing. Never bring up something which you can't explain, because your reader will figure out that you are hazy on the topic. In addition, as previously mentioned in this book, don't make obscure historical or literary references, and don't use foreign words which people don't know. Besides confusing your reader, these expressions will make you come across as being snobbish.

Another aspect of bad writing which consumes your readers' time and attention is to make them wade through long sentences which they have to reread for comprehension. Journalists strive to keep their sentences short for readability by, for example, cutting a large sentence in half. This can be done by starting a new sentence with the first word "And" or "But" followed by a comma. Starting a sentence with these words is often done by journalists (as I've often done in this book). Forget what your high school English teacher used to tell you. In addition, journalists often break up a long sentence by cutting it in half and starting a new sentence with the word "instead."

> Example:John White didn't attend the 2
> p.m. meeting on Saturday at Kinton City
> Hall. Instead, he attended the 4 p.m. meet-
> ing on Sunday at Cinder County Building.

Further, when mentioning dates, it's bad writing style to start off your sentence with the date. Instead, stick the date in the middle or at the end of the sentence.

> Bad Example: Thursday, Oct. 3, the direc-
> tors voted to increase the budget.

> Rewritten: The directors voted to increase
> the budget on Thursday, Oct. 3.

Numbers and dates used at the beginning of sentences often confuse readers before they've gotten the chance to reach the subject of the sentence.

In addition: do not use ordinal numbers with dates (i.e. "third"). Use Oct. 3, instead. And, always include the day of the week before a date so that your readers won't be inconvenienced by having to look it up. Further, avoid stating the year, if the event is taking place in the same year as the one in which you're writing.

Miscellaneous points on style include:

- Avoid saying "my point is" or "the moral of this column is." After all, your argument will naturally indicate your point or moral, if it is stated well. Also unnecessary, are phrases such as, "to my mind," "to my way of thinking," or "it's my opinion."

- Avoid complicated ways of saying things or even pompous ways. Instead of saying, for example, "John Smith does not hold this to be true," simply say, "John Smith doesn't believe this." (Note: use contractions whenever possible, such as "doesn't," instead of "does not" to keep the sentence crisp.)

- Avoid usage of outmoded terms or references. For example, don't call a child, "the little nipper," or "the little devil." Instead, try to be creative and invent a new term to describe something or someone. A child could, instead, be called "the little voice box."

- Avoid bad taste. Although this is a broad category, don't, for example, make ethnic or racial slurs. Further, don't imitate the way certain ethnic groups speak English when recreating dialogue or when quoting someone. In addition, don't use inappropriate terms: (i.e. Don't say "girl," if she's a woman.)

- Avoid using italics, capital letters, quotation marks, or exclamation points to emphasize certain words. Nor should you underline words for emphasis. These tactics simply can't compensate for the forceful words that you should instead be using. You can, however, put quotation marks around a word if you want to make certain that the reader knows, for example, that the person you interviewed used that particular word. (i.e. He believes antique collectors are "offbeat.")

- Avoid starting a sentence with "According to 'so and so'." It's better to end the sentence that way. Example: The athletic club is a good place to meet people, according to Jane Smith.

- If you want to start a sentence using a number, such as in "Thirteen state representatives attended," spell out the number, so the sentence doesn't look awkward.

- It's okay to end a sentence with a preposition, unlike what you were probably told in school. Example: His office reveals the high-pressured environment he functions in.

- If you do write a long sentence, to make it more readable, you can separate parts of it with a long hyphen (not a single one). This works especially well when there's a break in thought. (English teachers call these breaks " parenthetical expressions.")

    Example: There are those who would say, who have said many times as a matter of fact, that I am only fooling myself into believing this principle.

    Rewritten: There are those who would say—who have said many times as a matter of fact—that I am only fooling myself into believing this principle.

Part 2. Word Thriftiness

As a columnist, you'll need to economize on words, because you'll most likely be limited to a certain word count or word range. Most columns don't run beyond about 900

words. Because you must be word-thrifty, you must reread
your column several times. Each time, you'll be able to find
ways of paring your word count further, particularly with
factual statements. The most common way an editor can
spot an amateur writer is by how he wastes words.

As a rule of thumb, journalists avoid using multiple
words when a single word will do, and they leave out insignificant words like "the" and "that. " Let's take an example
of the former: why say, "at this point in time," when you
can simply say "now."

And, of course, redundancy is a no-no.

Study these examples, and let's pick out extraneous words:

(1) Store X is located in Fresno, California and Store Y is
   located in Claremont, California.

   Rewritten: Located in California are Stores X in
   Fresno and Y in Claremont.

(2) The following points are relevant in this issue: X, Y,
   and Z.

   Rewritten: These points are relevant: X, Y, and Z.

(3) Due to the above stated problems, guns should be
   outlawed.

   Rewritten: Therefore, guns should be outlawed.

(4) He was evicted as well as his neighbors.

   Rewritten: He and his neighbors were evicted.

(5) The meeting will be held twice in that evening at
   7:30 p.m. and at 9 p.m.

   Rewritten: The meeting will be held at 7:30 and 9
   p.m. (Note: no need to repeat "p.m." twice.)

(6) The terms of the contract call for a cost of living
   increase.

   Rewritten: The contract's terms stipulate a cost of
   living increase.

(7) One can interpret the drawings by identifying the
   four symbols represented in them.

   Rewritten: Interpreting the drawings involves identifying their four symbols.

(8) Away from his office, he is an amateur athlete who engages in a multitude of activities: tennis, golf, basketball, and football.

Rewritten: At leisure, he is an amateur athlete who plays tennis, golf, basketball, and football.

(9) The officials of the organization realized they had a problem, but they didn't know how bad the problem was or if it was a serious problem at all.

Rewritten: The organization's officials realized they had a problem, but they didn't know the extent of it.

(10) The tests are entirely voluntary on the part of the homeowners, and so far 39,000 of them have volunteered to take part.

Rewritten: The tests are voluntary, and so far 39,000 homeowners have volunteered to participate.

(11) The tests will be analyzed in order to look for patterns in behavior.

Rewritten: The tests will be analyzed to determine behavior patterns.

(12) Reduction of radon gas can be accomplished by using two basic methods.

Rewritten: Radon gas can be reduced by using two methods.

(13) Raised in Hockston, he attended Garibaldi High School. While a student at Garibaldi, he came up with this unique idea.

Rewritten: Raised in Hockston, he attended Garibaldi High School where he had this unique idea.

(14) In a short period of time, the shopping mall will be completed.

Rewritten: In about six weeks, the shopping mall will be completed.

(Note: Always be as specific as possible. "A short period of time" means little. Is that six weeks or six months? Also avoid saying "in the near future." Professional journalism demands specificity in statements.)

Other "Word-Thrifty" Tips

- Omit courtesy titles such as Ms., Mr., Mrs., or Miss before names. Most newspapers and magazines do
avoid them, although some of the more formal publications, such as the *Wall Street Journal*, include them.
Also note: after the first reference to a name, don't repeat the person's full name. Instead, use just the last
name. Example: Mary Smith is a good woman. Smith
does a lot of community volunteer work. (This is covered in detail in style manuals such as *The Associated
Press Stylebook and Libel Manual.*)

  If, however, you're writing about John and Mary
Smith, then on second and following references, you
could just say "John" or "Mary."

  Further, if you're writing about a child, on second
and following references, be informal and use the first
name only. Example: Joey Smith is five years old. Joey
likes to play with his train set.

- Avoid saying "whether or not." Just write "whether."
Example: It is unknown, at this time, whether the
measure will appear on the ballot.

- Though it's not necessary as a beginning columnist,
when you become a seasoned one, you may want to
browse through *The Associated Press Stylebook and Libel Manual*, a reference book available at your library.
An exhaustive work of a few hundred pages, the book
contains examples of all the various journalistic abbreviations and style points which many publications
follow. Frankly, the book is so exhaustive that very
few journalists take the time to memorize more than
a handful of basic rules. However, at least, it's some
sort of reference point. Recognize that "Journalese"
sometimes defies the rules of English.

Part 3. Refining Your Style

If you are going to be an effective columnist, first let your personality come through in your writing. This applies even if you are writing on a serious, informational topic. Second, be as conversational as you can be. Third, clearly illustrate to your reader what ideas you're trying to put forth by cultivating a knack for writing simply and using analogies.

This is a lot easier than it sounds. As we previously discussed, try to use similes and metaphors to convey an idea. In this section of the book, we'll be looking closely at similes, metaphors, and other types of useful linguistic tactics, such as a play on words, alliteration, hyperbole, epigrams, irony, and sarcasm.

First, in dealing with similes and metaphors, remember to use them sparingly, like salt and pepper ("like salt and pepper" is a simile in itself). If you don't use them sparingly, the reader will become so tuned into identifying your similes and metaphors, that he may lose sight of the information or basic ideas you're trying to convey.

Remember, a simile draws a comparison between two things through the use of "like" or "as."

Let's look at some specific examples:

- Her husband treated her like a housekeeper.
- The boss was like a drill sergeant.
- His voice was as smooth as that of a disk jockey.
- Her black leather skirt wrapped around her hips like the rubber swings we used to play on at the park.
- The sweat on his forehead dribbled like ice cream on a cone.
- My neighbor's daily visits are becoming as welcome as visits by the property tax assessor.
- He was puffing clouds of smoke like a muffler gone bad.
- The coffee was like sludge.

- She had about as much sex appeal as support hose fresh through the washing machine ringer.
- The lothario was as immoderate with women as a pie eating contestant is with sweets.
- She was as obnoxious as a party crasher who complains to the host about the bad food.

In formulating your own similes, do what I do: either keep lists of them as they come to you or take subject headings like "doctors" or "lawyers" and ask yourself what or who they are like. Later, fill in the blanks in your notebook when they come to you.

As for metaphors, although they also create a comparison between two different objects, they are a more subtle part of speech. Unlike with a simile, there is no use of "like" or "as," and the comparison appears to be a literally impossible claim.

Let's take these examples:

- His bickering was the relentless beating of a woodpecker. (Metaphor= bickering: beating of a woodpecker)
- The ladder of magazines allowed her to reach the top shelf. (Metaphor= ladder: magazines)
- The coleslaw floated in a sea of mayonnaise. (Metaphor= sea: mayonnaise)
- The storm of his divorce did have the positive aspect of making him a stronger person. (Metaphor= storm: divorce)
- The plaster was a blob of melted marshmallow. (Metaphor= plaster: marshmallow)

In formulating metaphors, practice looking at objects, and then thinking of things to compare them to. Gradually, you'll see how skillful you've become at creating them.

Besides similes and metaphors, also attempt to become adept at using puns (play on words) whenever applicable, because this is a common word exercise of columnists. (A pun is the use of a word(s) where it can have two or more different meanings.) Remember, too, that a columnist can cover one's negativity on an issue by using the lighthearted approach of a pun. Example: In business since 1975, this college-educated veteran prostitute is an entrepreneurial moonlighter. She maintains an open market with customers from all walks of life.

Let's consider some other puns:

- The house of David Lily is "The Lily Pad."
- He used a tonic for his problems: gin.
- During hard times in the fishing industry, the fishermen's safety net is tuna.
- He came up sevens in the lottery: $7,777,000.
- She looked at her bank statement and saw red. Her account was $500 overdrawn.
- The hairdresser's shortcut to business success was in giving her customers the blunt style.
- At his driving exam, he got the green light: a perfect score.
- The U.S. Postal Service has given its stamp of approval to postal increases.

Besides the previous techniques, you don't have to get fancy. Three effective parts of speech for columnists are, quite simply, verbs, adjectives, and adverbs.

When we observe things or when thoughts come to our mind, often we verbalize them in the simplest of ways. However, in your writing, strive to express these thoughts in the most picturesque way possible. If you are having difficulty, of course, you can use a thesaurus, but usually, this is unnecessary.

Let's consider an example. If the car had bumper stickers on it, was it decorated with bumper stickers? Plastered with bumper stickers? Studded with bumper stickers? Get the idea? Always look for more precise verbs. Remember, using a particular verb, rather than a general one like "had," gives your reader an exact picture of how you feel about the stickers and what they did to the car's appearance, without your having to say to the reader, for example, "They looked yucky." So, be a skilled writer by not hitting your reader over the head with such blatant statements as the latter—statements which don't give your reader a precise visualization of what you're trying to describe.

Similarly, with adjectives, move away from using general ones and strive for picturesque ones. Telling a reader, for example, that "the mobile home was unpleasant" does not give a clear mental image. How was the mobile home unpleasant? Was it sterile? Undecorated?

Further, move away from common adverbs. Instead of saying, "the book was very funny," ask yourself if "very" can be replaced by "heartily" funny or "irreverently" funny? You can always find a more specific adverb.

In your column, you can keep up a brisk, lively beat by using a succession of a particular part of speech, such as a series of nouns or verbs, all in one sentence.

> Example: During her Saturday spree, the shopaholic purchased boots, bloomers, blazers, bonnets, bows, bracelets, beads, and buckskins.

> Another example: He was so rabid about money that he would hassle, hammer, and hoodwink anyone who had it.

Besides giving a lively beat to the examples above, the alliteration (repetition of the same consonants in successive words—"b's" in the first example, "h's" in the second example), also helps to emphasize the people's manias.

Moving away from parts of speech, let's get into more sophisticated literary techniques which columnists enjoy using. For example, hyperbole (an exaggeration made for comic effect) is commonly used. Though hyperbole is an exaggeration, at its root, there is logic and truth. You can formulate hyperbole from your own lists of daily observations, including your pet peeves. Once you look over your lists, it's easy to expand on them through exaggeration.

Here are examples of hyperbole which I've created:

- Why do bank tellers count back your cash lightning-quick?
- The teen-ager jacked up his truck to the high heavens.
- Everyone calls himself a consultant. Burglar alarm salespeople are "security consultants," department store apparel salespeople are "fashion consultants," and realtors are "relocation consultants." My plumber calls himself a "porcelain consultant."
- Car bumper stickers which say, for example, "I love my...," have gotten out of hand. I'm waiting for a sticker that says "I love my tarantula."
- Everyone flaunts the title "Dr." Pretty soon, I'll be dropping off my car for repairs at "Dr. P. L Gray III's Car Care Emergency Facility."
- I know that supermarkets are trying to be environmentally-conscious and avoid waste, but things have gone too far. Yesterday, I toted 25 canned goods to the checkout stand and the cashier, after ringing up the items, asked, "Do you want a bag for that?"
- I wonder why expensive car manufacturers are putting out station wagons? I'd hate to see a kid spill a peanut butter and jelly sandwich in a Mercedes Benz station wagon. And, what next? Kids eating graham crackers in a Rolls Royce station wagon?
- I hate supermarket cashiers who smack cans of food across the price scanner and dent them. The other day, my can of pop looked like a can of sardines after the cashier got through with it.
- These days, school principals are so intimidated by parents, that I've known some to lock themselves in restroom cubicles to avoid speaking to irate parents.
- Dry cleaners will never admit to having ruined your clothes.Yesterday, the dry cleaner ruined my pants after they blew out of his delivery truck and he ran over them. Then, he told me the pants were expertly

cleaned by a revolutionary pressing technique.

- So few things in life are free, that many people, when hearing of a free offer, are hit with a freebieitis attack. People get involved in collecting trinkets or sending away for them, even if they are not remotely interested in them. Today, my neighbor answered a classified ad to send away for a free toothpick.

- Picture this: you've gotten your new phone installed. The thrill of the first ring! You feel like a somebody again. No, it's not a friend, not even a wrong number. It seems someone at the phone company has leaked your unlisted number to pick up a few bucks on the side. This time, it's a Hare Krishna calling.

- We live in a society where everyone, no matter, how lowly their occupation is, sticks the word "professional" in front of their job title. I've seen resumes stating "Professional Carryout Clerk" and "Professional Grocery Bagger."

- I went to a car dealership to look at the new car models. I was just planning on browsing, and I told the salesman that I was not ready to buy. After I sat behind the wheel of five cars, the car salesman said, "The suspense is killing me." Then, he began to weep profusely and said, "If you don't buy a car right this minute, I won't be able to save you any money."

Besides hyperbole, another popular technique of columnists is to use epigrams, a form of satire which attacks vice or folly, with a turn of thought at the end.

Here are some I've created:

- Corporate public relations people are mostly friendly, upbeat, poised, and mostly evasive when you need the full story.

- Waitresses are usually bubbly, chatty, courteous, efficient, outgoing, and usually out on break when your order comes up.

- A jack-of-all-trades is often creative, industrious, flex-
  ible, and often looking for work.

Further, we shouldn't overlook irony and sarcasm as
other common forms of expression among columnists.
Irony is simply a means of expressing a thought contrary
to what you are really thinking. Sarcasm is a little different:
it can be stated ironically, but it is also cruel and biting.

> Example of irony: The job of a parking
> meter patrol person is highly-specialized.

> Example of sarcasm: City Commissioners
> have voted themselves only a five percent
> raise since our city began operating in the
> red. With commissioners' salaries upped to
> $75,000, they can sit down to Thanksgiv-
> ing dinner and eat heartily, while recently
> laid off city employees dine at the soup
> kitchen.

Syndicated columnists Mike Royko and Roger Simon are
great at irony. Royko is also known for his sarcasm, while
Simon is adept at understatement to cover his disgust or
outrage on an issue.

Since sarcasm is often hard for the novice columnist to
pull off, perhaps you should, instead, take a lighthearted
approach if you are commenting on social and political issues. Remember, through a lighthearted approach, your
reader will indeed regard you as being perceptive and your
columns will have a lot of impact on him.

As you've seen in this chapter, being a colorful writer is
much easier than you think. You don't even have to force
yourself after you get going. It will become second nature
to you.

Chapter 6

GETTING PUBLISHED

Part 1. Introduction

This chapter will deal with three basic components: where to submit your columns, how to make your columns presentable to an editor (or I should say, how to get your work even noticed), and how to get the editor to publish them. Included in this discussion is how to build your column exposure from one publication to many, either through self-syndication or through syndication. The former term means that instead of dealing with a syndicate to achieve national distribution of your columns, you yourself will market, distribute, and arrange for the publication of your columns to newspapers, magazines, and/or newsletters throughout the country.

As a regular freelance columnist, you're not going to make big money from any particular publication. If you intend to turn a profit, then you'll need to build a business from dealing with several publications.

What beginning columnists need to realize is that syndication is not necessary to become prestigious and earn some money. You can be a success, even if you don't become syndicated, by self-syndicating your column. Usually, self-syndication begins after you've been successful at getting a regular column placed in one publication over a period of time. Then, through self-syndication, you gradually build a marketing base so that you are selling your column at the same time to numerous publications which don't require an exclusive dibs to your column. Often, this means striking an agreement with newspapers, magazines or newsletters which don't have conflicting territories of circulation and/or audiences, and who don't mind duplicating your individual columns. Of course, if you break into such arrangements, you must clearly establish written agreements with the managements of these publications, spelling out that your column will simultaneously appear in such and such publications. Each time you think of adding on another publication, you should, if you're not sure, also check with editors who currently run your column if they think this new publication will conflict with theirs, audience-wise.

As with any venture these days, you need to start small and work your way up. Don't think that your excellent educational credentials will make you a shoe-in for a prestigious general interest publication like *The New York Times*. The bottom line is can you write effectively as a columnist.

By "small," I'm generally talking about starting out at the local level in a small publication like a weekly community newspaper or in a small regionally or nationally-circulated specialized newsletter. If self-syndication or syndication is your goal, you must, build up to it little by little.

Remember that many columnists only strive to appear in one publication, without even setting a goal of self-syndication or syndication for themselves. These one-publication columnists, nevertheless, enjoy a great deal of exposure and prestige. For example, some of the one-publication freelance columnists later get offered a staff columnist position at a large publication in their area. Realize that "small" doesn't mean insignificant, and it is in itself a lot of exposure for you.

However, even if you don't strive for national recognition through syndication, you might get there anyway and achieve success you never dreamed possible.

Generally, in order for you to get published as a columnist, no matter how small the publication is, you have to be offering your readership something. Although this sounds obvious, haven't you ever read your local paper and noticed columnists who write week after week and you wonder why they are columnists? They don't seem to be offering their readers anything. In fact, all they seem to be doing is just taking up space, as if the publication doesn't have anything better to run. Or, if they have nothing to say, maybe there's the other explanation for how they became columnists. (We talked previously about connections. The analogy might be, how do people in the job world get jobs which they don't have the qualifications for? Certainly, if you've ever been employed before, you've run into co-workers like this. The answer is, of course, that they know someone in a decision-making capacity, or are even friends with them. Yes, publications are no different. When you read through your local newspaper or even a nationally-circulated publication of some kind and suffer through some columnist's drivel, you can imagine that he must have known "someone" at the publication who allows him to inflict his godawful gibberish on the readership. As a lot of readers do, I've complained to editors about some of their columnists, and yet month after month, year after year, some columnists stay on, as if in perpetuity!)

However, if you don't have any connections at publications, then you better be able to hook editors to your columns. How do you do this? Start by asking yourself, "Why will my readers need my column?" Recognize that "need" is the word which is the key when you are marketing anything these days, whether it's a product or a service. As a columnist, you must be a marketer of what you write, because you are offering editors and readers a product. Think of your column as a product. If you're not prepared to do so, then you probably won't get published. You'll be just like a student I once had who enrolled in my columnist workshop. Alas, she told me she had accumulated a drawer full of columns over a seven-year period that she had never gotten published. Why? Because she never realized that she had to go out into the world and contact editors, either in person or at least, over the phone. Simply sending off columns in the mail usually doesn't grab the editor's attention. After all, editors are like any other working people; they are buried under a stack of papers, most of which they never read.

I'll also tell you the anecdote of another one of my students. He never got up the gumption to contact an editor, despite the fact that he was a very gifted columnist. So what did he do? He gave away his columns (yes, for free) over a three-year period to the newsletter of the writer's club he belonged to. What was the circulation of the writer's club newsletter? About 75 people. Not much in the way of exposure and prestige! Here was a man who was a better columnist than some of the syndicated columnists I've seen, and yet the world will probably never have the pleasure of knowing him and his work. All because he never had the will to market his writing.

You must have the will to market your column. If you follow the steps I'll be talking about in this chapter, you'll understand the world of publications and how it operates, so you'll have the know-how to get your work published.

As the marketer of your writing, what is the key word? I repeat, "need." How will you serve your readers? If you are a lawyer writing for a bar association magazine, why do your colleagues need your column? What are you going to offer them that they don't already know? New insights? A different perspective on issues? Ideas on how to drum up clients?

If you are a physician writing for a general interest publication, what is your column going to offer the readers? A different perspective on health care? Bold insights for consumers on how to deal with their doctors? Ideas on how they can take control of their own health? Are you going to warn them about unnecessary medical tests and operations?

If you are an investment counselor, how are you going to answer your readers' questions on how they can make money?

If you are a social worker, how can you give readers answers on how they can solve their family or marital problems?

If you are a career counselor, what will you tell your readers about how to solve their employment problems?

Remember, a lot of people don't have the financial luxury or time to seek professional help from financial experts, psychiatrists, and other counselors, so they look to columnists for some direction.

If, however, you would like to write a creative column for a general interest publication, you don't have to do the homemaker bit like Erma Bombeck. Instead, you could focus on a different segment of the population. What about the singles scene? Male or female, you could write a column about single life, and you can do what Erma Bombeck does: make your readership feel a little less lonely in its struggle with daily living. Show other singles that their insecurities and fears are typical ones for the single person. For years, the singles population has been growing, with increasing divorce and single people postponing marriage until later. Give your readership answers to how they can create a better life for themselves. Be a friend to them, one they've never met, but one who seems to be experiencing common problems. I always felt that when Anna Quindlen, columnist for *The New York Times,* used to write her "Life in the 30's" column, that she was good at being a friend to her readers. In writing a creative column, drawing from your life's experiences, can you brighten your readers' day? Make them chuckle through adversity?

Are you a retiree? Write a column for retirees or senior citizens about the joys and problems of getting older.

Remember, too, that in order for you to write for a specific audience, you must not only understand your audience and their problems, but you must respect your reader. That's right, respect your reader.

As a columnist, you don't have to give your readership advice or insights which are unique—that no other columnist in the world gives— though if you could come up with something unique (which is extremely difficult to do), you'd be highly marketable.

Often, local editors of small publications would prefer to run a local columnist who is a good writer on a certain topic than to get a syndicated columnist because the local readership enjoys reading local writers whom they can get to know or even run into at civic events, from time to time. So, if you are a local Bruce Williams type (syndicated business columnist), you are not necessarily competing with the real Bruce Williams for columnist space in your local publication. If you wanted to become syndicated throughout the country, however, then you would be competing with Bruce Williams. In the latter case, even if you do write on similar topics such as Williams does, ask yourself how you are going to be different from Williams. You could have a different angle or approach to columns in this subject area and you could demonstrate better journalistic writing skills.

As a columnist, you should learn to be as bold as an entrepreneur who is trying to determine what the public needs and how to give it to them. In the beginning, as we shall see, you probably won't be making a lot of money off of your columns. Therefore, at first, your goal should be to consider what you can offer the public that will make them want to read and need your column, and thus make you a success. Then, you can move on to large publications and command better compensation.

Part 2. The First Steps To Getting Published

As I've said before, it's not realistic for the average aspiring columnist to attempt to approach a syndicate, because he's never been published. If you have no record of cranking out a column on a regular basis, and you have no proven track record or references from an editor that your column appeals to the general public, then approaching a syndicate is like going hunting without a gun.

Your best bet is to start small like Erma Bombeck and Art Buchwald did— in a small paper.

Assuming you've identified the type of columnist you want to be, it is not enough for you to have cranked out one sample column. After you've written one sample column, you must toss around some ideas, and draw up a list of about ten other column topics. This doesn't mean that you must crank out ten columns now. Out of these ten column topics, you could narrow your list to about four or even five column ideas. This way, you can write about four more columns and present your prospective editor with about five column samples. I would not present any fewer than that, because you have to demonstrate to him that you can write well, and that you have the ability to sustain your momentum in coming up with interesting topics. Of course, you could submit more than five writing samples, but don't sacrifice quality for quantity. It's better to give the editor five substantial samples than seven samples, two of which are not good. In the latter case, the editor would figure that your quality would drop off as time passes. (Once you get accepted as a columnist, you should have a reserve of as many columns as possible, depending on how busy your schedule is, so that you won't be grubbing for topics and writing frantically at the last minute.)

Assuming that you are taking my advice and starting small, begin with editors whom you can approach locally and start with a weekly publication. Even a neighborhood newspaper will do. (If you start with a newsletter or magazine in your professional or hobbyist field which is located far away, start with a small publication.) What exactly is a "small" publication? If a publication is small, its circulation is about 10,000 or less. A mid-size publication has about 40,000 circulation, and a large publication has about 100,000 or more circulation. These are ballpark figures. Editors often multiply the circulation figure by four when they want to figure out the actual number of people who are coming into contact with the publication, since people may be exposed to it at a library, office, or in a home with multiple family members. If you want to find out the circulation figure of a newspaper, consult *Editor and Publisher International Yearbook* at your library. I'll list some other circulation sources. For example, *Gale Directory of Publications and Broadcast Media* gives the circulation figures for newspapers and magazines throughout the U.S.; *Standard Periodical Directory* gives the circulation figures for magazines and some newsletters; and *Oxbridge Directory of Newsletters* provides circulation figures for newsletters, as does *Newsletters In Print*. These directories are also extremely helpful in that they describe the publications in detail.

As a beginning columnist, don't be concerned about the quality of the publication, unless it's absolutely horrible, and you don't want your name associated with it. As long as the publication is halfway decent, consider it. Make sure you are familiar with the publication, and don't approach it if it already runs a column in your field, unless you know the columnist is due to leave, or you figure he is a bad one and may be replaced.

When you submit columns, always double space or even triple space them, to make it easy for an editor to read and even make notations. On the first page of the column, start halfway down the page, to leave space for an editor's notations to himself. In addition, don't use the block style for paragraphs, but indent for each new paragraph. (Remember to keep your paragraphs short.)

Further with each column, think of a snappy title or

"head," as a journalist calls it. The head should grab the readers' attention. It could even pose a question. To give yourself an idea of what kinds of heads are good, scan heads in newspapers, magazines, and newsletters. You'll spot some lively ones, and it's a good idea to clip them out and keep a file of the most clever ones which you can refer to for inspiration periodically. Of course, editors often change heads to meet space constraints, but it's good, nevertheless, to provide heads with your columns to show an editor that you are capable of attracting people's attention.

Besides a title for each column, what will be your general column logo? You absolutely must present a logo idea to a prospective editor to show him that you've really thought out your plan to be a columnist. Remember, the publication's readership needs to be able to easily identify and recognize your column as it pages through the publication each week, bi-week, month, or depending on how often your column runs. The editor may well choose to use a different logo than what you've proposed, but don't let that faze you.

You don't often see more than a three-word logo for a column. As with each actual column and title, give the readership a logo which it can easily understand. A reader may not even read your column, if your logo and column title are incomprehensible. Often, columnists choose a logo which is a play on words. Let's fabricate an example of a column logo. Say you are writing a column on roller derby racing. In this case, your logo could be "Rolling with the Punches." Or, you could even use "Steam Rolling."

With your five columns, it's essential that you include a short cover letter which will introduce you and your proposal as a columnist. Even if you are visiting an editor in person with your column submissions, you'll need a cover letter for the editor's quick reference at all times— days, even weeks or months later. Your cover letter should state your credentials (professional ones, if relevant, and any credentials which qualify you to write a column, such as accomplishments in your professional field, or publishing credits.) The letter should also state why you are writing such a column, and why there is a need for your column in this publication. In the cover letter, state the name of your column (logo), something snappy, of course; something that readers will remember.

Whatever you do, don't begin the letter by stating, for example, "My name is John Smith and I've been a lawyer for 20 years." (Remember, this is English composition style which isn't used by journalists.) Instead, show the editor your ability to grab his attention with your interesting style. Sometimes a question makes for a snappy lead sentence in a cover letter.

Let's consider this entire cover letter which I've fabricated:

> Dear Editor (refer to him by name):
>
> How do I go about selecting a good lawyer? When do I absolutely need legal advice and when can I get along without it? Do lawyers take advantage of their clients?
>
> These are just a few of the many concerns which people have today about legal services.
>
> As a local lawyer for 15 years and workshop teacher at local community colleges during the past two years, I've given hundreds of people advice on these and other issues, such as how to protect their interests when buying a home and a car, planning financially for their children's education, preparing wills, what to do if an insurance company rejects your legitimate claim, and where and how to seek specialized legal advice.
>
> In today's fast-paced, dog-eat-dog world, people find themselves in a position to need basic legal advice, but often can't afford it. Perhaps they can turn for advice to a lawyer-columnist in your paper—one, such as I, who has experience as a teacher in explaining issues simply and concisely. Your readership is savvy and could benefit from legal advice.

I'm enclosing five sample columns of "Legal Rap," which I've written to compliment the style and format of your publication. The possibilities of column topics in the legal advice area are abundant, and I would like to be a regular columnist for your publication.

I'd very much appreciate your taking a few minutes out of your busy schedule to look over my work. I'll be calling you in about a week to determine whether you might be interested in discussing my proposal.

Thank you very much.

Sincerely yours,

John Smith

Your cover letter and five sample columns are important. Don't bother with a resume. If the editor is truly interested in considering you as a columnist, he may ask for a resume. It's important not to give the busy editor a whole mess of papers in the beginning as this may deter him from even touching your proposal. Remember in your cover letter to summarize your key accomplishments in your professional field, or if you're writing a creative column, to stress your publishing credits or writing background. (In the latter case, if you don't have any, that's okay, but focus on why the publication needs your creative column.)

Above all, remember that with whatever type of column you write, in your cover letter, always stress why there is a need for your column, and why you think the readership will be interested in what you have to offer.

Besides a cover letter, if you have any published work in newsletters, newspapers, or magazines which may be relevant (except letters to editors), attach a few photocopied samples— your best ones. Staple your cover letter to your columns, along with copies of your published articles at the end. Number the second and following pages of each column (in the upper left corner) with your name beside each number, followed by the first few words of the column title, in case the staple breaks loose. Write "30" at the end of each column, signifying "the end."

Also, on the first page of each column, in the upper left corner, state your name, then on subsequent lines, your address, day/evening phone numbers, and finally your social security number (for payment, if the columns are run.) Your cover letter should also include this information in the upper left corner.

At a weekly publication, you should contact "the editor" or "managing editor." (Get the correct spelling of his name.) If the publication has both an editor and a managing editor, then contact the managing editor. Do not contact the person with the title "Editor and Publisher" because he is actually the publisher. (However, if the publication is so small that there is no person who is the editor or the managing editor, as in the case of some neighborhood papers and professional newsletters, then you should contact the Editor and Publisher.)

When I say "contact," I mean that you should actually drop in unannounced to the publication's office, if possible, and personally hand your cover letter and samples to the editor. (Obviously, you can't do this if you're, for example, submitting a column to a small newsletter far away.) Do not phone in for an appointment, because you'll never get one. Editors don't have the time to set aside a few minutes of their day for everyone who wants to see them. At a small publication, you'll walk in the door and often see the editor's desk. (Usually, he has no separate office.) Tell the receptionist you want to drop off "a few things in person to the editor." Take only one minute of the editor's time to state you who are and what your purpose is, and tell him you'll be calling him up in a few days or a week to check back with him. Keep your words brief so as not to allow him to launch into a pitch about how he's not looking for a columnist. After all, he may not be looking for a columnist, but if you're persistent and he likes what he sees of your work, he might quickly become interested.

The best time to contact an editor in person is 2 p.m. (This goes for newspapers, magazines and newsletters.) Avoid mornings, since editors are usually in meetings or are busy meeting deadlines. Even if editors take a late lunch, they are usually back by 2 p.m.

Remember, personal contact counts. You may want to call the publication shortly before you drop in to see the editor, just to verify that he is indeed in. Call up and ask to speak to the editor, and when the receptionist transfers your call and the editor answers, hang up! If the editor should step out sometime between the time you placed the call, and when you arrived at his office, then leave your columns and cover letter on his desk or with the receptionist and follow up with a phone call an hour afterwards to speak to the editor to verify that he received your columns. (It's essential to place this call to verify that he got your work and that he did, in fact, notice it on his desk.) Reiterate that you would very much appreciate his taking the time to look over your work, and that you'll be checking back with him in a few days.

Then, no more than a week later, call back, and reintroduce yourself as the person who dropped off the columns. (Remember that editors hear from a lot of people each week, so don't expect your name to click with him right off the bat.) Ask the editor if he's had time to look over your work. If he says he hasn't, tell him you'll be checking back with him in another week. Keep after him on a regular basis, unless the editor gives you an absolute "no." If, for example, you've talked to him twice, and he hasn't given you a definite answer, or if he says he's not interested "at this time," call back in a month to see if his situation has changed any. Also, take note of the fact that editors often hop along to new jobs, so if the present editor isn't interested in your proposal, maybe his successor will be.

Recognize that editors are generally aggressive people or at least they like those who are, so don't be shy about keeping yourself in front of them. If you're reserved by nature, that's okay, but try to assume an aggressive demeanor when dealing with editors. Personally, I wouldn't waste more than two months in pursuing a particular editor. Always keep an ongoing file of prospective editors at various publications to contact. And, don't simultaneously pursue general interest publications in the same circulation area, or special interest publications such as newsletters in a professional field with the same audience, because if two publications with conflicting audiences accept your column, the editors probably wouldn't want you to write for both. (There is usually competition between similar types of publications which either circulate in the same area or have the same audience.)

From the beginning, be businesslike in your contact with editors. Don't ramble on and on. Always have a brief little script ready, if necessary. A lot of editors are abrupt, so don't abuse what little patience they have. As an added note, always keep copies of your work and correspondence that you've dropped off to editors (or mailed off) because they are notorious for losing and misplacing papers. Even if you provide them with an SASE for the return of your work (I would do this), don't automatically expect them to return it. You may have to hound them to return it, since they'll probably misplace the SASE.

Whatever publication you contact, I caution you not to discuss payment in your cover letter. After all, why discuss payment, if you don't even know if they'll be interested in what you have to offer? As far as pay, you'll probably be in for a rude awakening. I should tell you that at weekly newspapers, staff writers who work about 65 hours a week make about $14,000 or $15,000 a year: starvation wages, no doubt about it. What about freelancers? One can only shudder. At a small newspaper, you may be paid some nominal sum such as $5 or $8 per weekly column ($10 if you're lucky) or you may even be giving it away for free, in the beginning, until your column proves popular. Yes, it is ridiculous. Also take heed: inflationary increases are usually foreign to editors who deal with freelancers.

There are, as you've probably seen, metropolitan weekly

newspapers, free to the public, which are heavy on entertainment features and columns. These weekly papers have
a circulation in the few hundred thousand to several hundred thousand range, thus making them large publications. Even so, these large weeklies pay their columnists token sums, not necessarily any better or very much better
than the small weeklies. In addition, large weeklies are
much more difficult for the columnist to crack than small
community weeklies, due to the competition to write for
them, since they are so popular with writers for the exposure they offer.

Say, you are in a professional field where you are used to
commanding $100 or more an hour for your advice. I
would guess that the prospect of getting paid literally pen-
nies for a column which you will spend a fair amount of
time producing will sound pitiful to you. However, the issue is, are you willing to do it for the exposure—the exposure which will indirectly lead to more money with in-
creased clientele becoming familiar with you? Also,
consider that you'll undoubtedly become well-known
enough to be asked to give paid speaking engagements to
civic groups.

(I should mention that depending on your particular
professional field, a regular column in a trade journal prob
ably wouldn't make you rich, either. Moneywise, an occa-
sional article or guest column published in that publication would probably pay more than what you'd get per
column piece as a regular columnist.)

If a small weekly, large weekly paper, small newsletter, or
a small magazine likes your work, but it can't afford to pay
you much or even anything, you could ask the editor if, instead of payment (or, in addition to little payment), the publication could run a free ad for you on a regular basis to advertise your services or any products that you offer in your
professional field. If, for example, you give workshops, you
could advertise those, or if you're a published author, you
could advertise your book. If you're a homemaker writing a
creative column, you could get a free ad announcing your

garage sale, your need for a baby-sitter, a repairman, or any other need. (Whatever type of columnist you are, ask for a large display ad.) Editors of small newsletters are especially agreeable to this type of arrangement.

Before you give a column away for free, make sure you've checked out all possible paying publications. Personally, if I were a beginning columnist, I would only give away a column for free as a last resort. Just about any publication can afford to pay $10 per column running each week, if it really wants your work. If you're providing an informational column on your professional expertise, it's hard to justify giving away information for free, unless it's for a limited trial time only, or unless you're getting a lot of exposure from a free ad that the publication gives you. If the editor keeps harping on "free," you could, for example, agree to such an arrangement for a few months only. After a three-month trial period, if he still won't pay, then take your talent elsewhere.

Once your column proves out in a small or large weekly, you could leave it and offer your experience to a large metropolitan daily newspaper in your area or region. You could negotiate for more pay, such as $25 per column per week. If your column proved to be really hot stuff running in the metro daily, you could even weasel $40 per column per week, if the paper had your column on an exclusive basis, with no other publication running it. Obviously, you're still cringing at this. However, you must recognize that editors can buy the columns of famous syndicated columnists for a lot less than even $25 from the syndicate. As I've said before, if you're a talented local personality, however, editors will often opt for your work, as they might feel that as a local personality, their readers can relate to you more than a syndicated columnist.

Remember that with practically any publication, your arrangement will be a casual one with no contracts or guarantees. The editor will rarely, if ever, want to enter into any kind of commitment with you. By the same token, you will want to be free to leave and move on to bigger things.

Therefore, any contracts should not be entered into, in this case. Just decide on whether you'll be able to write the column weekly, bi-weekly, or monthly. You must commit yourself to this. You should maintain all ownership rights to your work. Affix your copyright notice. For example: Copyright 1993 by Tom Tutts. Discuss this with the editor.

Always stress the positive with an editor. If he does like your column, ask him what the pay range is for columns, and tell him you'd like to be at the top of the scale. Tell him that since you have knowledge of the journalism basics and your column wouldn't require major editing, you're worth every penny he can afford.

If you've been writing your column for a small publication for six months or a year, and you've gotten some exposure, you'll probably want to move on to a bigger publication. Or, if not, at least you'll be thinking of getting a pay increase. As a columnist, the burden of proof will be on you to show an editor that your column is successful, so that he'll want to keep running it and offer you more money, or so that you can take your success to a larger publication and get more exposure and money. Of course, often your editor will get "Letters to the Editor" about your column, and he'll know, therefore, that at least people are reading it. The important thing to remember about being a columnist is that it doesn't matter whether readers love or hate your column, as long as they are reading it. You'll probably never be dropped from your columnist position if people hate your column and complain to the editor about your views. (Unless your views are totally bizarre, obscene, vulgar, or insulting to a certain race, creed, or color, you usually don't have anything to fear.)

Realize that if people hate your column and you get hate mail, this often works in your favor! Generally, all that editors care about, is that you've come up with a way to get people to read your column, no matter what they think of it.

It is largely up to you to measure reader interest. If, for example, you are writing an informational column on a weekly basis, after the first two months, you could advise readers that in a few weeks, you'll be running a question and answer column, so they can write in with their questions now, in care of the publication. (Alert your editor that you're doing this to measure reader response, and alert your readers that not every question will be run—only a select few, and that remaining ones may be answered in future columns.) Obviously, if you are flooded with mail (count the pieces and show them to your editor), there is interest and a need for your column. Note: if you are dealing with a publication far away, the mail room will forward your mail, and you may want to photocopy pieces of your mail to send to the editor.

An alternative to this response method is to offer your readers a sheet of free informational tips about a certain topic of your expertise, if they send you a self-addressed stamped envelope in care of the publication. Count the pieces of mail, show them to your editor, and also keep the postmarked envelopes for your file. Of course, if you elect this latter method, you are getting into spending your own time and money to get this information together and mail it off. Don't go overboard with your time and money. The reason I suggest informational tips is to keep your time and money to a minimum. Don't offer lengthy information on a complex topic. Limit it to one sheet of paper. Also, recognize that you must promptly respond to each reader's request for information, otherwise the publication will be flooded with phone calls, asking, "Where is the material I sent for?" In this case, you'll not only lose popularity with your readers, but also gain the ire of your editor! Incidentally, or not so incidentally, you should affix your copyright to any information (free or otherwise) that you are giving out. If you don't, your readership can copy it because it will be considered in the public domain. Simply write at the end, for example, "Copyright 1993 by John Doe." Also note, that in going into the mailing of free information, don't forget to use this opportunity to include a few sentences at the end of your free information to advertise your professional services, along with how readers may contact your office.

To test your readership with a creative column, you could, for example, ask your readers to write in to you about the funniest thing that has ever happened to them at work, or something simple that they could easily respond to and that relates to your column in some way. Tell your readers to limit their response to three sentences, so you don't get a novel from them, and so that you have space to include various responses.

Besides for the purpose of tracking your readership, you should always keep a record of readers' correspondence (stapling the postmarked envelope to the back of the sheet of paper) in case you reprint a reader's remark (with their written permission), and there's some question about what they stated. There may arise a question about who wrote what and what was actually published. In the latter case of asking readers to report the funniest thing that ever happened to them at work, it's a good idea to ask them to enclose their phone number, so if need be, you can call them and verify that they indeed submitted the piece.

Depending on how much mail you receive, on a regular basis, such as at the end of each week or every two weeks, show your editor the pieces of mail. For the editor's perusal, you can even highlight with marker pen any favorable statements which your readers have made about your column.

When I was a staff columnist, I would even show my editor negative statements about my column which readers wrote in with. In fact, I remember many staff writers would read aloud their hate mail for the enjoyment of the rest of the staff. You'll find, as a columnist, that you'll often receive witty comments from your readers, whether you agree with them or not. In fact, with your readers' written permission, you could even reprint their comments about a particular column you ran. I'm sure that in reading your favorite columnists, you can recall that they ran a column devoted solely to readers' comments made about a particular column they previously wrote.

In general, perhaps a way to really garner popularity as a local columnist, is to allow the public to meet or see you at as many events as possible. You'll find that the more social, charitable, and civic events you get involved in locally, the more people will feel like they know you and gravitate toward reading your column. Therefore, try to have your hand in a lot of activities.

As I've said, you may not want to start out "small" at a weekly. If you feel you are, for example, well-known in your city, professionally or socially, and you live in a large metropolitan area, you could approach the metropolitan daily newspaper or a city magazine. With a daily newspaper, realize that each section of it has its own specific editor. Therefore, if you are writing a column on daily living, you would approach the "Living Editor," "Lifestyle Editor," or "People Editor." Note: different publications use various names for their lifestyle-oriented section, but at any rate, you will be able to recognize the lifestyle section.

At a large daily paper, if you wanted to submit an entertainment column, you would approach the entertainment editor or arts editor. Or, if you wanted to submit a travel column, you would approach the travel editor. Get the idea? There's a separate editor for everything at a large daily paper, so you should not approach the managing editor, unless you know him really well and want to use him as a connection.

Let's take some more examples of contacting specific editors at large daily newspapers. Got a business column? Obviously, you'd contact the business editor. Got a health column or self-help column? You'd most likely contact the lifestyle editor. Got a gardening or cooking column? If so, you'd contact the lifestyle editor. Sometimes metropolitan daily newspapers have a food section insert (tabloid) each week in the newspaper. If you have a cooking column, you may want to contact the editor of this tabloid.

As I've said, as a freelance columnist at a large daily metropolitan paper, you could likely get $25 per column each week, depending on how much the editor wanted your work, and how much different what you're offering is from what they could get from a nationally-syndicated columnist. Perhaps, if you so desired, you could even work your way into a staff columnist position on the newspaper, with your column appearing a couple or three times a week. As a staff columnist on a large daily paper, you could even get paid $60,000 a year. See how the financial picture would change from a freelance columnist to a staff columnist at a large daily paper? (Note: do not confuse a large metropolitan paper with a small daily newspaper which circulates in a mid-size or small city. Large metropolitan papers have a few hundred thousand circulation, and today, they are almost always owned by large newspaper chains. The large metropolitan newspapers can afford to pay staff columnists a lot of money, depending on whether they want to or not— that is, depending on your popularity and/or reputation. For example, if you are a well-known published author in the business or investment field, your pay could be negotiable.)

Remember, however, that small or mid-size daily papers with circulations less than 100,000, could even offer you as little as a weekly community paper as far as freelance pay. And, these publications usually prefer their already existing staff reporters to write columns periodically, than to hire a full-time staff columnist.

When in doubt about the circulation figure of a newspaper, consult *Editor and Publisher International Yearbook*. In most library systems, just call your local library and the reference librarian can quickly look this information up for you.

If you want to find out the name of the specific editor to reach at a large metropolitan newspaper, simply call up and ask the receptionist. Or, often in *Editor and Publisher International Yearbook*, editors of certain sections of each newspaper are listed. In recent editions of *Gale Directory of Publications and Broadcast Media*, the publication has begun to also list the names of departmental editors at newspapers.

At a large metropolitan daily paper, do not forget about the regional Sunday Magazine supplement. Often, here you will find a regular columnist or two, though often they are staff writers. Even if there are no columnists here, you could propose a regular column that would interest the Sunday Magazine editor. Subject areas are varied. I've even seen regular health columns and interior decorating columns running in the Sunday Magazine. Here, with such a large circulation of its Sunday edition, you may be able to negotiate about $30 for each weekly column as a regular freelance columnist. A guest columnist might get as much as $100 to $150 per one-shot column. Why do they pay more per one piece? Because they often prefer the diversity which different writers offer. (Incidentally, large trade publications pay comparably for guest columns.)

Often, you may find that your column is suited to more than one section of the metropolitan daily newspaper. If so, first try one section, and if the editor rejects it, try the editor of the other section.

Remember, that contracts at large metropolitan daily newspapers are also extremely hard to get. After all, staff members never even get them unless they have an executive position, such as managing editor—and maybe not even then. So, as a columnist, your column would really have to catch on and you would have to be a really exciting addition to the paper in order to get a contract.

At large consumer type of magazines, you will have difficulty getting on as a regular columnist, because the decision is made by several editors— not just one. You could first pitch the idea to the "articles editor" or some specialized editor, if there's a particular section you'd like to write for. However, it takes a great deal of time before editors get together and jointly decide. One editor may like it, and the rest may not. Here, the pay would be negotiable and varies greatly with each publication, depending on the type of column you're writing. An informational column written by a medical professional who has published a book, for example, would command more money than what a local metro daily paper would pay.

Again, as a regular columnist you should have the publication agree that you hold ownership rights to the column, if in turn, you agree that you will not sell your column to another publication within its circulation area. You should also be free to sell your column to a publication with a different audience, such as a specialty magazine or a trade magazine, if one wants it as a reprint. (Note: even if you give away a column for free to a publication, make sure that the publication doesn't have the ownership rights. Affix your copyright to it. Always confirm (in writing) that you want to be able to submit your column to other publications outside of its circulation area, or to an unrelated publication with a different audience.)

With a confirmation (in writing) as to the rights of your column, have your agreement signed and each party should maintain a copy of it.

Part 3. Self-Syndication

If you've had some experience writing a column and you want to expand beyond your local general interest publication, or if you're writing a column for a trade publication and you want to expand and offer your column to other trade publications, then self-syndication is a great way to go.

Let's take some examples of the above. Say your column has been running in a large daily newspaper in San Francisco and you feel your column is of interest to other large cities in California, you may, then, decide to contact large daily papers throughout California to sell them your column. (Remember: small weekly and small daily newspapers are very localized, so they would usually only be interested in local columnists, unless you were a famous columnist.) Now, let's take the trade publication example. Say you are a professional speaker and you are writing a column for a trade publication for public speakers .You might later decide that you want your column on good speaking skills to run in a variety of trade publications where good speaking skills are needed by professionals— from a teacher's journal to an insurance salesperson's journal. Through self-syndication, you would take it upon yourself to contact and sell your column to each individual (non-competing) publication.

Your first step in self-syndication is to research (through directories listed in the appendix of this book) what possible publications your column could run in. As I've mentioned before, look through *Editor and Publisher International Yearbook* for newspapers; *Standard Periodical Directory* for magazines and some newsletters; and *Oxbridge Directory of Newsletters* and *Newsletters In Print* for newsletters. *Writer's Market* is also a good directory primarily for listing magazines which specifically seek freelance material.

Always, I mean always, when you approach editors, let them know about your self-syndication plan to contact publications of non-competing circulation. Send them samples of your published columns (a few of your best ones), telling them in a cover letter that your column is now running in "X" publication, and that you'd like to branch out and get your column running in theirs, too. Give them statistics on how much reader mail you've gotten during the past year or send them a few sample copies of some readers' letters. In addition, you could even have the editor of the publication your column is currently running in, write a letter of reference for you (or you could provide the phone number of your editor for reference purposes.) In the former case, editors usually don't have much time to write letters of reference, so you could even offer to write your own letter of reference and have your present editor sign it. Why not? I've done this a lot through my career. If the editor doesn't like certain parts of your letter, he can edit it, and you can retype it for him to sign.

When you begin to sell in large volume to many publications, you will obviously be making more money than you were before. Don't get excited, however. You will have to incur money when self-syndicating, and you will have to spend a fair amount of time doing it, depending on how large an enterprise it becomes.

Sometimes, though not usually, publications may want you to send them camera-ready material. This could get expensive. If some of the publications you happen to select require camera-ready material, you may want to reconsider whether you want to deal with them or go with other publications.

Even if the publications you contact don't require camera-ready columns, you'll, nevertheless, have to incur the money in photocopying and mailing your typewritten columns.

However, let's say you have a column running in your local daily newspaper on running a home-based business. If you want to self-syndicate it to just one daily in each of the other 49 states, for example, with your column running in 50 papers every two weeks, you could make some money to make the time and expense worth your while. Though now that you are self-syndicating, a column which an editor might have paid $25 for, if his publication was the only one running it, will most likely pay you much less for it. Further, as a self-syndicator, consider that you are most likely getting into full-time work which includes marketing, distributing, and bookkeeping.

Remember that in order to self-syndicate on a large scale, you must be well-organized. At the beginning of each month, the publications in which your column runs, will want your supply of columns for that month. So, particularly if you are submitting columns to publications cross-country, you'll have to be especially efficient in making sure your columns reach their destinations on time.

You should mark each column in the sequence it should run. This is important if you have, for example, written a column which should run on a timely basis: a column about Christmas shopping should obviously run before Christmas. Or, as another example, you may want to announce as soon as possible, a question and answer column to which readers need to submit questions. Therefore, the column that contains this announcement needs to be run first.

When you mail your columns each month, include an invoice with them so that the editor can pass it along to the accounts payable department. (Get invoices at a discount office supply store, the kind in triplicate, so that if you are not paid on time, you can send a duplicate invoice to the accounts payable department.)

Generally, publications pay freelancers once a month. After you've been accepted as a columnist, you should verify when you can expect to receive your payment.

As a self-syndicator, you are the decision-maker as far as your marketing strategy. You can keep contacting publications indefinitely, or at some point, you can decide that you're tired of marketing, distributing, and collecting bills for your own work, and that you're successful enough to take a crack at scoring with a syndicate.

Remember, that even though you won't be earning much money at self-syndication, the positive side is that since you are marketing and distributing your own column, you don't have to split your column pay with a syndicate.

Since self-syndication could easily become a full-time job, make sure you can afford to devote all your energies to it. If you're not sure you can afford the time to market and distribute your column, then don't self-syndicate, but focus on selling your column to one publication, and then moving on to a better one periodically.

Self-Syndication Summary Tips

- Consider self-syndication after you've gotten used to the routine of being a columnist.

- Offer proof to prospective editors about the success of your column. Send copies of your best columns, those which you received a lot of compliments about, or those which you received a lot of reader-mail about.

- Your cover letter to editors should include mention of your self-syndication goal; statistics on the reader-mail you've gotten, sample quotes from readers' letters, or sample readers' letters; and an editor's recommendation, if possible, or his phone number for reference purposes.

- Only approach editors of publications where your type of column would fit it. If you are going outside of your own region of the country, you've got to be writing columns which appeal to people in other parts of the country.

- Don't approach general interest publications which have overlapping circulation areas or special interest or trade publications with the same audiences.

- Enclose a self-addressed stamped envelope for the possible return of your unaccepted material. Remember, it involves time and money to make more copies of your columns, and publications do not absorb the cost of returning unsolicited material. (Even with an SASE, some editors won't return your material. In this case, don't waste more money in writing back and re-submitting an SASE. It's probably best to let it go.)

- Follow up with editors with a long distance phone call a week after you think they have received your material. If the editor says he may be interested, but needs more time to think about it, ask when you can check back with him, and call back at that time. Editors play hard to get, so take the initiative at all times. If the editor says he's interested, ask him to drop you a line telling you what he feels he can offer you as far as pay and as far as a trial run period. (Do not make any decisions about offers over the phone. Always tell the editor you'll need a few days to reflect.)

- If an editor is hesitant to take on your column, but you really want your column to be accepted by his publication, you may want to ask him if he'll try out your column for a couple months without pay to see if the readership in his part of the country likes it. However, don't enter into an agreement of this kind unless you really want the exposure that this publication could give you. After all, you've already proven yourself as a columnist in one or more publications, so don't be too quick to offer freebies.

- Confirm in writing the payment you'll receive and when it's due; frequency your column will run; deadline for submitting it; and the word count or approximate word count. Confirm that either you or the publication can decide to terminate the arrangement at any time, for any reason. Further, confirm ownership rights to the column and the fact that you are not offering the column to competing publications.

- Keep a bookkeeping system of who owes you what and when. This will be easy for those computer owners who have an accounting program. If you don't have a computer, keep a calendar of payment due dates and also follow-up dates to send (postcard) reminders to accounts payable departments, if payment is late.

As for self-syndication to metropolitan daily newspapers and mid-size daily newspapers, realize that practically all of them these days are part of newspaper chains. This is good news for you, since once you've gotten yourself published as a columnist at one of them, then you've gotten your foot in the door as a columnist at others of them in the chain. By reading *Editor and Publisher International Yearbook*, you can identify the chain that a particular daily newspaper belongs to and then scan the directory for other papers of that chain. Or, simpler yet, if you are currently writing your column for a daily paper, ask the editor of that newspaper if it is a part of a chain and which other newspapers in the region or throughout the country are a part of that chain. When you contact those affiliated publications, you would obviously mention early in your cover letter that you're currently writing for another paper in its chain and that you're enclosing published samples in the hopes that you may also be considered as a columnist for this paper. In this case, it would be especially helpful to enclose a letter of reference from your present editor. However, keep in mind that these editors in different parts of the country often favor local talent unless you are really offering them something they can't resist. Be irresistible!

Although you may have your foot in the door with affiliated papers of the same chain of the newspaper which you currently write for, don't limit yourself to these. If, for example, you started out writing your column for a metropolitan daily newspaper, you may want to self-syndicate to a few more metropolitan papers throughout your region of the country or beyond, which have no affiliation to the one you currently write for. Your next step might be, for example, to contact the editor of a metropolitan daily in a neighboring state. And from there, contact other metropolitan publications in states neighboring the previous one, then ones throughout the U.S.

By now, you probably realize that I seem to focus on getting your work into newspapers over magazines, if you have a general interest column. You bet I do. You should consider newspapers first, because newspapers have more space for columns than magazines and newsletters do, and columns are run more frequently in newspapers, simply by virtue of the fact that newspapers come out more often than these other publications do. Also, these days, magazines, in particular, seem to be getting stingier with space for freelance material. Newspapers have more sections where your column could conceivably run, compared to magazines and newsletters. Another plus with newspapers is that since they come out more frequently than do magazines and newsletters, you won't be waiting as long to get your material published. After all, if your column was appearing in quarterly magazines and newsletters, you'd get awfully impatient waiting to see your column in print. Lastly, newsletters and magazines seem to cease publication more frequently than do newspapers.

What do you do when you're tired of beating the bushes, contacting editors and distributing your columns? Say you've been successful as a self-syndicator, now what?

Part 4. Pros And Cons Of Syndication: The Big Time

Maybe you've gotten sick of self-syndicating your column and contacting editors to market your work. If you've been successful at getting a string of publications to run your column, and now you want a syndicate to go all out and sell and distribute your work to several dozen publications or more, maybe you should take the plunge.

Let's discuss the basics of syndication. Remember that syndicates are the columnists' agents who promote and sell columnists' work to publications. If you feel you're at the point where you want to deal with a syndicate, rather than be your own agent as a self-syndicator, realize that syndicates want to be paid well in order for them to represent you. With a syndicate, you'll have to sign a contract. Before signing any contract in the publishing business, I would urge you to have an attorney help you. Caution: publishing law is very specialized, so just any old attorney won't do. If you live in a large metropolitan area, you could most likely find a publishing attorney, an intellectual property attorney, or a patent attorney or entertainment law attorney could assist you. (A patent attorney handles a variety of matters besides trademarks, and an entertainment law attorney works with musicians and writers alike. If you live in a smaller metropolitan area, a patent attorney or entertainment law attorney may be more readily available.) At any rate, these specialized attorneys are usually more expensive than the average ones. Since publishing contracts tend to have so many intricacies, a specialized attorney is essential to have to protect your interests.

There are a handful of major syndicates in the U.S. and most are owned by large media companies. For example, some of the large ones are: King Features Syndicate, Tribune Media Services, Universal Press Syndicate, Los Angeles Times Syndicate, Washington Post Writers' Group, and the New York Times Syndication Sales Corp.

Of course, contracts are always negotiable, depending on how badly someone wants what you're offering. However, remember, as with any form of publishing, the writer, unless he's famous, does not have a whole lot of bargaining power, and the publisher, or the agent who reaches the publisher (in this case the syndicate), usually has the upper hand. With a syndicate, you would most likely have a contract which would give it at least 50 percent of your column sales to publications, less expenses. What are the expenses, you ask? There is the expense of marketing, advertising, producing, and distributing your typeset, camera-ready column, billing each publication, and sending you a royalty check each month. Since this runs into money, when done on the large scale that syndicates do it, the average syndicated columnist whose work appears in a few dozen publications, comes away with $20,000 maximum, and probably much less a year. Sure, nationally-syndicated columnists like Mike Royko who are household words, pull in several hundred thousand a year plus thousands of dollars for lectures, and radio and television appearances. However, the really famous columnists like Royko are represented by major syndicates. You should recognize that there are a lot of small syndicates which pay very little.

With any syndicate, you should always maintain ownership rights to your work. Further, you should not sign more than a five-year contract with a syndicate, thereby being free to switch syndicates after this period.

Make sure your contract states that you are to receive a report periodically of all the publications which carry your work and how much they pay the syndicate. You have a right to know not only who's running your column, but you should be able to verify the syndicate's correct payment of your royalty. In your contract, you can also stipulate that you can audit your account at the syndicate to show that you are serious about correct payment. Unfortunately, this would be expensive to enact, especially if you would have to locate a CPA in the syndicate's area to do this.

Your contract should also stipulate how much money the syndicate will devote to advertising and promoting your column, and whether all of these funds or part of them will be deducted from your payment.

Further, your contract should stipulate what will happen in the event of a lawsuit arising from your column. Will the syndicate cover you, for example, for libel or invasion of privacy? Depending on the type of column you write, there are numerous pitfalls. Will you be held harmless?

Trying to get rich as a columnist is probably like trying to win the lottery. There are over a thousand syndicated columnists in the U.S., and many of them are small potatoes, moneywise. Read a directory called *BPI Syndicated Columnist Contacts* which lists more than 1,600 major syndicated newspaper columnists in over 30 categories. There is also *Editor and Publisher Annual Directory of Syndicated Services* which lists syndicates serving newspapers in the U.S. and abroad, and you should browse this, too.

When considering the number of syndicated columnists, it's easy to understand how you could be syndicated in a few dozen publications through a small syndicate, and earn very little. Sorry to burst your bubble, but reaching the point of syndication doesn't necessarily mean "Easy Street," as you may have thought. If you regularly peruse large and small newspapers from throughout the country (you can send away for them through their circulation departments), you'll begin to see syndicated columnists in dozens of subject areas, from those who deal with child rearing to those who deal with leisure time activities. However, these columnists aren't the Mike Roykos, the Ellen Goodmans, and the Erma Bombecks as far as pay. They are usually the poorly-paid syndicated columnists.

What your lawyer can do for you is to negotiate a deal, based on the success of your column which you've already achieved on the local level, for example. What the syndicate eventually agrees to depends on how popular it thinks you're going to be, given its experience with other columnists which it has represented, and also based on its intuition regarding the trends and fads in this country. There has to be a market for what you write, and syndicates must determine how much editorship and readership demand there will be for your column.

Of course, what you'll end up doing is querying a lot of syndicates and selecting the one which gives you the best offer. (Or, it's possible that you'll only get one offer.) Among the best sources to find information on the numerous syndicates in this country are *Writer's Market, Literary Market Place, Editor and Publisher International Yearbook,* and *Gale Directory of Publications and Broadcast Media*—reference books found at your library.

Approach a specific person at each syndicate with the same written submissions as we've discussed before. Although syndicate people are horribly busy, try to reach them by phone, a few days after you think they've received your material. Keep the call brief. Just verify that they remember getting the material. After that, wait a few weeks for a written reply. If you don't get one, phone again. The decision-making process takes time because various people at the syndicate must approve of you as a columnist before you're accepted.

The people who are employed by syndicates constantly read newspapers and magazines from throughout the country. They keep their eyes and ears open for columns which they feel are suitable for syndication. (However, if you're writing for some obscure publication, I wouldn't be too hopeful that a syndicate will discover you.)

I must confess, I've seen more than a few syndicated columns which are poorly written, but at least they are written about subjects which are popular with the general public. Sometimes, syndicates even seek out people who already have a national reputation in their field, and they ask these people if they'd be willing to write a column.

Syndicates get thousands of submissions each year, no matter how small the syndicate is, even if it's a Ma and Pa operation. After all, most everyone is hungry to get published. Obviously, syndicates don't even have the time or manpower to plow through all these submissions. It's no wonder, then, that out of all these submissions, only a minute fraction of columnists will ever be picked up by a syndicate.

I firmly believe, as I've stated before, that if you feel you are truly interested in being selected by a syndicate, it would benefit you to go the route of self-syndication beforehand, so that you can approach a syndicate with a record of success as ammunition. Again, present yourself to a syndicate with the same materials that you would submit to an editor, as we've already discussed.

You've got to have built up a reputation so that syndicates will pay attention to you. And, consider this: if you've really built up a chain of publications which carry your work through your self-syndication efforts, this would obviously increase the chance that a syndicate will spot your work and approach you.

Some people mistakenly think that syndicates only handle daily newspapers. However, some also handle weekly papers, magazines, and newsletters.

Syndication can be an exciting venture for you, if you also consider the fact that unlike you, a syndicate has connections all over the country, and can, therefore, more easily place your work. There are about 1,586 daily newspapers in this country, and thousands of general and special interest magazines and newsletters. A lot of ground to cover!

You must realize, however, that all is not peaches and cream for the top nationally-syndicated columnists. Just think about how the top nationally-syndicated columnists have to entertain such a broad audience—geographically, social classwise, agewise, and political groupwise. They can't limit themselves to writing for any small group, but must focus on the interests or issues which concern practically everybody. Syndicates, therefore, desire columns with broad appeal because this country is so diverse.

As for the managements of publications who buy columns from syndicates, they do so if they feel those columnists are offering talent or expertise that doesn't exist in their area. In addition, a newspaper subscribing to a syndicated column almost always has exclusive rights to its publication in its community or immediate area.

Besides the exposure you get with syndication, I must caution you about some negative aspects of it. Syndicates, whether large or small, tend to be impersonal with their columnists. That is, given the fact that they represent a large number of columnists, they tend to focus their marketing efforts on the columnists who are their most popular ones. They, then, keep pouring their money into marketing those columnists to more publications, and the other columnists fall by the wayside. Interestingly enough, some syndicated columnists, particularly those with the small syndicates, go back to self-syndication after their syndicate agreements cease. In marketing their own columns, these columnists feel they make more money than what the small syndicate offers them.

The world of being a syndicated columnist is much like that of being a published writer of books. The author finds that the book publisher pumps his money into marketing the best sellers and the other books often lose popularity because they aren't being sufficiently marketed.

Part 5. Being A Guest Columnist

If you are interested in simply being a guest columnist, submitting a (one-shot) column here and there, to different publications on different issues, whenever you feel like it, this could prove lucrative to you, if you focus on nationally-prestigious publications like the metropolitan newspapers of major U.S. cities. They often pay a few hundred dollars. Besides guest columnists who write for the Op-Ed pages of newspapers and magazines, there are also those who write creative personal essays (often nostalgic or humorous ones) for the Sunday Magazine supplements of newspapers. These writers of creative columns also find that they can make a few hundred dollars off of each piece.

In the former case, you usually must address yourself to specific issues which the newspaper or magazine has focused its news stories on lately. In the case of creative columns, you must carefully tailor your piece to the style and general areas of interest of columns previously run, so you must get your hands on back issues of the publication at your local library (or through inter-library loan, if possible.) *Writer's Market*, an annually-updated reference book at your library, is especially helpful in identifying Sunday Magazine supplements for which you may write guest columns. (With its listings of thousands of publications with descriptions of each one and what freelance material each publication seeks, you can locate publications to write regular columns for, too.)

In being a guest columnist, always read nationally-prestigious publications at your library and note which ones tend to run guest columns on a regular basis next to the editorial page. Of course, first check out the large metropolitan newspapers located in your state. If you find these publications generally run guest columns only of famous people or well-known leaders in your area, don't waste your time submitting columns to them. However, many of them run columns by the average citizen. In many metropolitan newspapers, there are guest columnists who are the average Joe Citizens who have never been published before, but who have something interesting to say. A unique directory which lists leading national newspapers with opinion-editorial pages, offering guest columnists a forum to showcase their views and ideas, is *National Survey of Newspaper "Op-Ed" Pages*. It is available through Communication Creativity, PO Box 909, Buena Vista, CO 81211.

Of course, your local community weekly paper, if you approached it with a community issue, would probably run your guest column on the Op-Ed page. However, it might not offer you any pay.

On the creative end, you can even spot a guest column on a weekly basis in the Living sections of some large metropolitan papers. Even magazines run guest columns, particularly the lifestyle ones.

As for news magazines, for many years, *Newsweek* has run a column by a different person each week. Here again, it's usually Joe or Jane Citizen who speaks out on an issue of his/her choice, in its "My Turn" column. The column, located toward the front of the magazine, runs about 1,000 words. The pay is $1,000! Besides, the prestige is outstanding! If the column is really good, from the exposure you get, you may even be offered a staff columnist job by an editor at some publication who runs across it.

Very often, guest columns in prestigious publications aren't written very well. However, if you have an opinion on a timely and/or controversial news topic, and you write with passion and force, you can have a crack at getting published. The editor, in this instance, may just take the time to polish it up a bit.

The trick to getting a guest column published in a particular publication is to read the back issues of that publication at the library. See what kinds of topics are usually run. Many prestigious publications take first-time writers.

With guest columns, sometimes you are asked to give all rights to the publication. Unless you are paid a few hundred dollars or more, try to sell for first rights only, so that you may later be able to resell the column as a reprint, or reuse the material in book form. Don't be afraid to negotiate.

Part 6. Additional Tips

In this section, I'd like to provide you with some miscellaneous tips which will help you write and get published with the least amount of hassles as possible.

- When writing a column which gives vital information which, if misconstrued, could have disastrous results (such as a health or legal advice column), you should have an agreement with an editor that if he edits your work, you'd like to see the copy before it goes into print. Sometimes, of course, rewording changes the meaning of information and some editors aren't always careful when they edit. (Also, some editors are just plain bad.) If you have a contract with a syndicate, you could have your lawyer write in a clause to the effect that the syndicate should consult you before any editing changes are made.

Of course, it's always a good idea to write your column as clearly and succinctly as possible, so that there are no statements which an editor or syndicate might mistake the meaning of and touch up.

• As mentioned before, if you really want to be a seasoned journalist and use abbreviations and style elements in your writing which working journalists use, you may consult *The Associated Press Stylebook and Libel Manual*. The book is quite extensive, and even most working journalists only master a fraction of all the rules. Yet, I'm sure as you've read newspapers from time to time, you've noticed some odd capitalization or odd ways of abbreviating words or punctuating sentences which don't conform to the rules you learned in English class. "Journalese" sometimes breaks the English rules you learned. Either out of curiosity about "Journalese" or if an editor changes your style and you wonder why he did, you may want to consult this book at your library. I would also consult this style book if you use a lot of numbers in your writing in order to learn how to abbreviate large figures. (Business columnists should refer to the book.) Whatever style rules you follow in your writing, be consistent, so, for example, you don't capitalize a word one time, and later in the same column you capitalize it.

Incidentally, this manual was devised by The Associated Press, the largest wire service in the United States. The AP, with bureaus in each state and around the world, sells articles to publications which subscribe to its service. For example, you may note that your local metropolitan paper which doesn't have reporters in another part of the country, runs AP articles from that part of the country.

- As I mentioned previously, you should come up with your own logo to accompany your column, and it should be short, sweet, and snappy— two or three words. And, what about a photo to accompany your logo? You can submit your photo to an editor or syndicate, once they've accepted your column, if they want one. (A local publication, however, may want to have its staff photographer take its own photo of you.) About your photo, avoid the stereotypical columnist pose of the hand holding up the face or the index finger poked into the face. These columnist poses are probably getting tiresome for most readers to see. Be yourself. Consider that most of the time, you probably don't have your hand fixed into your face. Just a straight shot of you is preferable.

Besides your logo and photo, you may even want to suggest to an editor or syndicate that some art work (a symbol, for example) identify your column. Editors and syndicates always appreciate good ideas from columnists. For example, if you are a horticulturist writing a gardening column, you could have a design of a flower next to your logo and picture. Obviously, you have to wait for your column to be accepted before you get to the stage of discussing a graphic symbol (and your photo) with the editor. However, when you are accepted as a columnist, the editor would be glad to have a staff graphic artist design a symbol for you, if relevant. (Large publications have graphic artists on staff, but small ones don't.) For a small publication, you could even find and use your own symbol through a "clip art" publication at your local art supply store. If you've never heard the term clip art, you've probably seen it being used with large ads in newspapers. Clip art can be used by anyone for publication without copyright permission, and you'll find an assortment of designs and symbols to meet your needs. You can browse an art supply store and purchase a book of clip art for only a few dollars. In fact, even if the publication you're writing for is small, it has a supply of clip art in its advertising department which an editor would probably allow you to peruse.

- As for getting published, often in small, local publications, and once in a great while, in large publications, you'll see an ad that they are looking for a regular columnist. Unless you're really interested in the publications, my advice is not to respond to these ads, as these publications are swamped with replies. No matter how good a columnist you are, it's often very difficult to get your foot in the door because of the volume of replies they receive. If you really like the publications, you might think of approaching them at a time when the columnists have been there for some months and you think there might be a chance that they might leave.

- After you sell yourself to an editor, or after syndicates sell your columns to many publications, don't think that success is automatically yours. Your job has really just begun, as you must continually please your readers!

Part 7. Publishing Summary Tips

- Don't overlook obvious markets. Obvious markets are community papers in your area. Even if you don't live in a certain community, you can try that community paper if you're employed in that community and are well-known there. If you're a professional and you'd like to write for your peers, don't forget associations you belong to, for they have newsletters. Or, you could write a column for a trade publication in your professional area of expertise. The latter could be well-paying, depending on the profession it represents.

If you're a homemaker with a creative type of column, join a local writers' club and ask that it run your column. Of course, you wouldn't get paid for this, but this would be an easy way of getting started if you're intimidated about getting your feet wet at the local paper. Don't stay too long, however.

- Do your homework on publications. This usually involves investigating reference material at the library, besides scrounging up sample issues of the publications. For a complete listing of reference material which lists publications, see the appendix of this book. *Writer's Market*, for example, not only has listings and descriptions of general interest magazines, but specialty and trade publications, too. It also targets what freelance material these publications seek. *Writer's Market* also lists if the particular publication gives a free sample that you can send away for, or that you can get for a nominal charge. Now, this is important because if you are serious about becoming a columnist, you should build your own little library of publications. You can also get publications for free at libraries which have a publication exchange rack. If your local library doesn't have an exchange rack, ask your librarian if the library can start one. Remember, librarians are very accommodating to patrons. An alternative is that you can buy recent back issues of magazines at a used book store or rummage sales. (Caution: make sure all magazines and newspapers you look at are recent, because publications often change format, even after a six-month period.)

Writer's Market also lists which publications send out free writer's guidelines for the asking. These will identify what type of material the publication seeks, who the target audience for the publication is, and what the pay scale for guest columns is. Writer's Guidelines give even more details on the particular publication than does Writer's Market.

Writer's Market targets a few thousand magazines which specifically seek freelance material of every kind. However, you should realize that the majority of the many thousands of publications in this country will consider freelance material, if approached. At your local library, the current copy of this reference book is an annually-updated one and does not circulate. But, the previous year's edition most likely circulates, and that is worth your time checking out.

If you peruse or regularly read a publication which you think you'd like to sell your column to, even if that publication doesn't currently run columns, approach it with your idea. Most publications are open to any good idea from a freelancer. If you are interested in selling your column to a newsletter, consult *Newsletters in Print* and also *Oxbridge Directory of Newsletters*, both of which list newsletters according to their subjects of specialization— in such categories as newsletters for women, for writers, for senior citizens, and practically every subject imaginable. Often, sample copies of newsletters are available for free or for a nominal charge, so check these directories to find out if there is a charge.

Also consult your local libraries for regional writer's directories which focus on all publications in your area of the country. For example, in my neck of the woods, the Northwest, an exhaustive directory listing all newspapers, magazines, and newsletters, and even writer's organizations is *Writer's Northwest Handbook*, published by Media Weavers, 24450 NW Hansen Rd., Hillsboro, OR 97214. For California and Hawaii writer's markets, consult *California and Hawaii Publishing Market Place*, and for markets in the Southwest, consult *Southwest Publishing Market Place* for its coverage of Nevada, Utah, Arizona, Texas, and Colorado. The latter two Market Place directories are published by Writers Connection, 1601 Saratoga-Sunnyvale Rd., #180,

Cupertino, CA 95014, and they include newspapers, magazines, newsletters, and writer's organizations.

By doing your homework on publications, I also mean that you should check your local library for back issues of community papers and metropolitan newspapers in your state, and also regional and nationally-circulated daily papers. Your local library will also carry a selection of magazines, both general interest and specialty. If you live in a small community and your local library is small, ask your librarian if a certain publication is available through inter-library loan. Or, visit a local college library. (In some states, the public colleges and universities allow citizens to check out materials if they have a valid driver's license, so you don't need to be a registered student.)

It's important to browse newspapers and magazines to see what kind of columns, if any, they run, so you can determine if there is a gap your column would fill. By browsing, you may get an idea for a column which you could submit to a publication— something it doesn't already have which you've seen in another publication, for example. Remember, if you ever lose the address or phone number of a publication, rather than make a special trip to the library for it, contact the reference librarian at your local library and chances are, he will quickly look through a directory to find it. Writers are busy with little time to waste!

- Study your markets well. Know your competition. An editor who has the Erma Bombeck column probably wouldn't drop it for your column (or run your column, too) unless you really had a fresh angle. So, don't try to duplicate what a publication already has. Either come up with a truly original idea for a particular publication or ask yourself, "Does my column fill a gap in this publication."

- Don't forget to browse tobacco shops for specialty magazines. Check these out for major regional and national newspapers and magazines which are of high quality.

- Unless you're involved in self-syndication to many general interest publications, don't mail off a column to a publication you've never seen a copy of. When starting out tapping individual publications, be somewhat familiar with each publication you're targeting. You need to establish what its needs are in relation to what you are offering. If you cannot find a copy of a particular publication at your library, then send away for a copy through the circulation department of that publication. Call the circulation department first to inquire about the cost. (When self-syndicating to general interest publications such as daily newspapers, you can try the shotgun approach for expediency. After all, you'd have to read the paper each day of the week to really assess what kinds of columnists were represented, and this wouldn't be practical.)

- As a regular columnist, avoid large general interest magazines, until you've become well-established. Remember, the decision-making process at these magazines usually tends to run for several months, as a variety of editors ruminate whether to even run a major freelance article. So, given this fact, you can imagine that deliberations on whether to have a regular columnist would be lengthy. If you're a beginning columnist, you'll need the immediate rewards and encouragement of getting published within a reasonable amount of time. So, personally, I would avoid the large general interest magazine route until you're proficient.

- Avoid mailing off your column to a general interest publication not in your immediate area unless you've first been published locally. It's very difficult to get published when you mail off material to a general interest publication, because you don't have personal contact with the editor, and it's hard to follow up and track him down by phone. Mail columns off, after you've established a track record close to home, unless you're dealing with trade or specialty publications or unless you are submitting a one-shot guest column.

- When you approach an editor, make sure your supporting materials to your column are relevant. Do not show an editor, for example, poetry which you have previously gotten published. That would be irrelevant. Also, a published letter to the editor would not impress an editor, either, since it's not an article. Always consider what is relevant. After all, an analogy is that someone applying for a job as a physician would not tell his prospective boss that he once held a summer job at a cannery.

All editors care about is solid relevant experience such as journalistic experience in writing articles. (If you wrote for your college newspaper, you might throw that fact into your cover letter to show that you have an inkling of what journalism is all about. Or, if you studied journalism in college, you could mention that, too. However, I wouldn't provide copies of published articles from your college newspaper days unless they were award-winners.)

If you're writing a column on physical fitness and you teach aerobics classes, that is not only relevant, but essential to mention. If you're a psychiatrist writing a self-help column which you'll submit to a general interest publication, and you've had articles published in a trade journal, mention this in your cover letter. However, if these articles are too technical, don't submit copies of them. (Incidentally, editors refer to articles as "clips.")

If you want to get a cooking column published locally, and you're a cooking teacher who has taught classes or given workshops at community colleges, that would impress an editor because you have some name recognition among the public.

Of course, relevant related experience is essential, but the bottom line is to offer good columns which can solve your audience's problems or inform them about something, and your being able to express your facts and ideas in a comprehensible way.

- Be persistent and keep submitting your column. In the publishing field, rejection is very common, no matter how good you are at what you do. Don't forget this. Also, a lot of editors aren't good and don't recognize talent when they see it— yes, even at prestigious publications.

However, it's been my experience that the more persistent you are, sooner or later, someone will give you a break with your first chance upon which you can build on for better opportunities.

- Make contact with editors any way you can. Befriend local editors, for example. By this, I mean, contact editors at local publications with ideas for articles which they can put their staff to work on. Make a practice, for example, of dropping off a note to them about an interesting person you know whom they could have a staff writer write an article about. Or, write them a note about an interesting organization, club, or activity which they could have a reporter follow up on. Editors are always in need of ideas. (Include your phone number so they can call you, if they need to ask you a question about this.) Or, write to editors, in letters to editors, complimenting them on a particular article or issue they ran.

As another suggestion, learn to write feature articles yourself and submit them on a freelance basis. (To learn to write features, read my book, *Beginners' Guide to Writing and Selling Quality Features*.) This way, editors will get to know you as a writer.

If you do any of the above, little by little, these editors will remember your name, and you can then present yourself as a columnist. (Note: do this with trade publications and trade association newsletters, too.)

- Always keep in touch with editors. Once you've got a

regular column going, keep in touch with editors every two or three weeks, especially if your column runs weekly. Do this, even if it means, making a long distance phone call. Ask an editor if he is satisfied with your column, and if you can do anything to improve it. Or, as I mentioned before, notify him of reader response to your column. (If you make a long distance call, leave a message if the editor isn't there, and mention when you can be reached. Because you are a regular columnist, he can call you back and foot the bill, unless it's a small publication which has a limited budget.)

- Editorship is a revolving door, so be prepared. Every six months or a year, you may be dealing with a different editor who has taken over and who may have a change in mind—one who may even want to drop your column. That's the worst scenario. The best scenario is that every two years or more, a new editor takes over as your supervisor. If a new editor comes in, he may decide he doesn't like your column, or that he doesn't want a columnist at all. That's life, unless you're lucky enough to be at a large publication and have a contract, and that's rare.

On the flip side, an advantage to being a freelancer is that if an editor is bad, you can up and leave. You're not tied down like a staffer is.

Another plus side to the aspect that editorship is a revolving door is that if you originally submitted your column to a publication and the editor rejected it, if a new editor comes in, you can resubmit your column. This time, your column just may click with the goals of the new editor.

- Test your column ideas out regularly on people you know. Other people can offer you great input on your ideas, helping you to refine them or give you perspective on a new angle. Their comments may also lead you to other ideas for columns.

Further, testing your ideas out on others will give you a certain amount of confidence when you see your column in print. You'll be confident in your ideas, knowing that your column appeals to at least some people, and you'll know that it is written comprehensibly. This is especially helpful if you start to get flack from your readership. You'll know that at least some people thought your column was good.

- Don't let your quality slip. The minute you drop off in producing quality columns, you'll begin losing readers and that could lead to your being let go as a columnist. Each of your columns should be good. Readers want to know that they can count on you to be consistently good.

- Keep reading other columnists. Always clip out what you like in other people's writing. You'll improve your own style.

- Keep a notebook logging your columns. You must be organized and keep a list of each published column by title, general subject matter (a two-sentence description of its content), along with where and when it was published. Also, keep a file of each column after you clip it from the publication, and write the date right on the clipping. Clippings should be glued to a sheet of paper so they can easily be found while plowing through a file. (Get a subscription to the publication so you can clip your column. Obviously, if you're syndicated or self-syndicated it isn't feasible to clip all your columns. Just one will do.)

Make a couple of photocopies of each column, and keep one of the copies under a different roof (i.e. your office or a bank safe deposit box). You want to keep your published work for life, not only as a record of your accomplishment, but also in the event that you go seeking a better columnist position and need copies of your clips to show. The original copy can always get lost or destroyed.)

- Keep track of your writing expenses. Expenses include: paper, postage, typewriter or computer maintenance, notebooks, travel miles/gas to visit an editor or interviewee, and magazines/books purchased on writing or about your professional field. You may be able to deduct these expenses, depending on how much you earn as a columnist, for example. For IRS purposes, keep copies of correspondence to and from publications, even rejection slips, to prove that you are actively engaged in writing as a business.

I keep receipts for everything: from postage stamps, subscriptions to newsletters, office supply store items, to photocopies of my written work. You do the same. Even keep a notebook in your car to keep track of mileage and parking meter money spent.

Postscript

Before I turn you lose as a columnist, I still have a lot to say. Above all, keep in mind that the only way to get published is to get something down on paper. Don't be paralyzed by fear! Remember, most of the columns published these days are not great ones, but the columnist had the determination to get them done and market them.

Stop finding excuses not to write. Write down on your calendar that your first column will be finished by the end of such and such a day, and that the next day you will contact two editors. Keep a schedule and stick to it. As a professional writer, even I need to keep reminding myself to write down my writing and marketing goals on my calendar. Yes, I'm a procrastinator, and what I usually do to avoid writing is to become active in a local writer's club and volunteer my time. Shame on me. Don't you come up with your own excuses.

Sometimes, too, you procrastinate because you fear success. Though this is a hard concept for many people to grasp, it's true that some people fear the changes that suc-

cess might bring into their lives: loss of family time together, travel, decisions to make about new opportunities,
to name a few. Are you one of these people? If so, admit
you are and deal with the problem now. What is the alternative? Not to write? To do something else?

If you do decide to write, scared about writing your first
column? Just start writing, no matter if it's completely disor-
ganized, and has misspellings and bad grammar to boot.
Just get something down on paper, and worry about revis-
ing it later. You see, once you get past the first step of getting
something—anything down on paper—then you have at
least some motivation to gear up for a few revisions.

Yes, it's hard for all writers, even professional writers, to
sit down and write. How many times in writing this book
did I avoid sitting down and writing by coming up with
other things to do, even cleaning the bathroom! Yes, at
times, I'd rather do just about any unpleasant task than
write.

The solution: when you procrastinate, fill yourself with
positive thoughts about writing, such as visualizing yourself as a published columnist. If you believe you will be
published and visualize yourself as a successful columnist,
you'll program yourself into making it a reality. Visualize in
detail: the recognition you'll get, people coming up to you
in the street, and your friends congratulating you, for example. I'm sure everyone has visualized attaining
something in their lives that they wanted, and they, indeed, got it. I've done this. It works. It does. I'm a realist,
but I also think big!

Often, as a columnist, you'll find it frustrating (amid
your other duties) to find the time and peace to do your
writing. For example, if you're a mother, you should have
a baby-sitter come into your home and she can play with
your kids downstairs while you write upstairs. Or, you can
escape to the quiet of the public library.

I had a male student who would leave his family occasionally, and check into a hotel to do his writing. My personal solution is to find a local convent or retreat house

and rent inexpensively by the weekend, week, or month. Even if you're not Catholic, convents and retreat houses need the money, so they'll except you. Best of all, meals are prepared in the dining hall, so you don't even have to worry about cooking food. No phones ringing, either.

Once you've found a quiet place, set up your regular work schedule. However, before starting your writing each day, take a walk in the fresh air, not only to get your mind working, but also because exercise puts you in a positive, upbeat, energetic, and motivating mood. Regularly scheduled breaks are also important.

Another tip to getting started as a columnist is to join your local writer's club to get moral support from other beginners. Through other members, you can find out markets for your writing or editors that others have had success with. You can also get your work critiqued.

No writer's group in your area? Start one. Post a note on your local library's bulletin board. Ask the librarian if you can use a room there, one night a month, once you've located other writers.

Further, another motivator in getting started as a columnist is to make yourself feel like one. How? You can spend a small sum, as little as $10 for 500 business cards at a discount office supply store. Have your name, phone, address, and title of "Professional Writer" imprinted. These business cards help editors, interviewees, and acquaintances reach you. With the latter, tell them you're looking for writing ideas and that they should feel free to contact you.

Remember that the average columnist won't get rich from writing columns, so he must look toward his column writing as a springboard to very lucrative activities such as lectures, giving corporate workshops/seminars and consulting, and getting a book published or producing an audio tape to dispense professional information. These activities could result in thousands of dollars of income each year. As mentioned before, the exposure a columnist gets sometimes leads to getting a future book published.

To use your fame as a columnist toward related money-making activities, be sure to read two books by Jeffrey Lant: *The Consultant's Kit: Establishing and Operating Your Successful Consulting Business* and *Money Talks: The Complete Guide to Creating a Profitable Workshop or Seminar In Any Field.* Further, don't forget the classic book on speaking, written by Dale Carnegie: *The Quick and Easy Way to Effective Speaking.* Of course, there are dozens of other books on these subjects, so check your local library index.

Just an added note: if you do wish to pursue the lecture, workshop/seminar circuit, you can start by getting some experience at community college or four-year colleges in their evening extension division. However, only get your feet wet here, because they pay poorly. I know this firsthand, as I've been a consultant and lecturer at colleges from coast to coast and have made little money at it, considering the time it took to prepare for the engagement. The solution: once you've gotten experience and a reference, go for speaking engagements at large associations, civic groups, corporations, and trade conventions. That's where the money is.

One final thought on being a writer. One of the frustrating aspects about being a writer is that once you see your piece in print, you think of things you forgot to include, or ways you could have stated things better. Remember, this comes with the territory. I've never met a writer yet who said, "My piece was perfect." Therefore, learn to live with what goes into print, and use it as a learning experience to improve on subsequent pieces. No one will ever be a perfect writer, but you can become awfully good.

Appendix

Selected Columnists And Their Anthologies

Following are a few of my favorite columnists and their best anthologies, though you may find you'll want to read more anthologies by them and those of other columnists, too.

- **Russell Baker**, syndicated columnist of *The New York Times*, has a sophisticated, somewhat erudite style. He writes with clarity on topics, such as urban life, politics, aging, his frustrations with modern society, and nostalgia. He often uses irony and parody. His columns often reflect pessimism and melancholy concerning daily modern life and its ironies.

Baker, Russell, *All Things Considered*, Philadelphia: Lippincott, 1965.

Baker, Russell, *No Cause for Panic*, Philadelphia: Lippincott, 1964.

Baker, Russell, *So This Is Depravity and Other Observations*, New York: Congdon & Lattès, Inc., 1980.

- **Erma Bombeck** is well-known for her comic insights on everyday living. Most people identify her with columns about the plight of the homemaker, though her topics have been varied in recent years. Bombeck is gifted at using hyperbole, and she has a succinct, hard-hitting style.

Bombeck, Erma, *Four of a Kind*, New York: McGraw-Hill, 1985.

Bombeck, Erma and Bil Keane, *"Just Wait Till You Have Children of Your Own!,"* New York: Doubleday & Co., Inc., 1971.

Bombeck, Erma, *Motherhood The Second Oldest Profession,* New York: Dell Publishing Co., 1983.

* **Jimmy Breslin**, a New Yorker, writes about modern society, social and urban issues such as the plight of the poor, political issues, and New York neighborhoods, among varied topics. He uses techniques of the novelist to bring news events alive, making up characters in his columns. He often gets his column ideas from the street. He uses irony, humor, and hyperbole, and demonstrates great reportorial skills.

Breslin, Jimmy, *The World According to Breslin,* New York: Ticknor & Fields, 1984.

* **Art Buchwald**, columnist of the political scene in Washington, D.C., writes with a great deal of wit and insight. He's a great satirist. Even if you're not a political buff, you'll find his columns thoroughly enjoyable because they say a lot about modern society, particularly social issues in the U.S.

Buchwald, Art, *Have I Ever Lied To You?,* Connecticut: Fawcett Crest, 1969.

Buchwald, Art, *"I Am Not A Crook,"* Connecticut: Fawcett Crest, 1975.

Buchwald, Art, *Laid Back in Washington,* New York: G.P. Putnam's Sons, 1981.

Buchwald, Art, *"You Can Fool All Of The People All The Time,"* New York: G.P. Putnam's Sons, 1985.

* **Christopher de Vinck** writes columns about life, mainly those about his memories and reflections on parts of his own life. He deals with the importance of good values, family, marriage, poignancy of life, lone-

liness, and illness. He has written guest columns in *The New York Times* and the *Wall Street Journal*, for example. He's a sensitive, thoughtful writer who writes poetically. By profession, he's a high school English teacher. I highly recommend him to those who wish to write creative columns.

de Vinck, Christopher, *Only The Heart Knows How To Find Them*, New York: Viking, 1991.

* **Ellen Goodman**, syndicated columnist of the *Boston Globe*, often covers women's issues with logic, insight, and great skill. She uses picturesque language and is a word smith.

Goodman, Ellen, *Keeping in Touch*, New York: Summit Books, 1985.

Goodman, Ellen, *Making Sense*, New York: The Atlantic Monthly Press, 1989.

* **William Geist** is a writer whose columns appear in *The New York Times*, and he is well-known for his writings about eccentric people and the offbeat in New York.

Geist, William E., *City Slickers*, New York: Times Books, 1987.

* **Bob Greene**, syndicated columnist of *The Chicago Tribune*, writes about everyday people and the famous alike, and also about social and political issues and trends. He uses good observation skills, and often gets his column ideas from everyday situations which he encounters.

Greene, Bob, *American Beat*, New York: Atheneum, 1983.

Greene, Bob, *Cheeseburgers, the Best of Bob Greene*, Boston: G.K. Hall, 1986.

Greene, Bob, *Johnny Deadline Reporter: the Best of Bob Greene*, Chicago: Nelson-Hall, 1976.

- **Lewis Grizzard**, syndicated columnist from the South, writes humorously about modern society and his own life in a down home style. He often covers the American psyche, everyday problems, and Southern culture.

Grizzard, Lewis, *When My Love Returns From The Ladies Room, Will I Be Too Old To Care?*, New York: Ballantine Books, 1987.

- **Anna Quindlen**, syndicated columnist of *The New York Times*, now writes about issues in the news. Formerly, she often wrote in a personal style about daily life and her perspectives on growing up, family, marriage, and women's issues. She writes with humility, and this is one of her strong points.

Quindlen, Anna, *Living Out Loud*, New York: Random House, 1988.

- **Mike Royko**, syndicated columnist of *The Chicago Tribune*, is famous not only for his columns about Chicago, but certainly for his social and political perspectives about life in the U.S. His outspoken style of sarcasm, scorn, wit, and irreverence is unparalleled. Anyone would agree, he's the most outspoken columnist around!

Royko, Mike, *Like I Was Sayin'* ..., New York: E.P. Dutton, Inc., 1984.

Royko, Mike, *Sez Who? Sez Me*, New York: E.P. Dutton, Inc., 1982.

- **Roger Simon**, syndicated columnist, formerly of *The Chicago Tribune*, covers social and political issues in a highly-skilled manner, through use of humor, irony, understatement, and hyperbole.

Simon, Roger, *Simon Says*, Chicago: Contemporary Books, Inc., 1985.

- **Calvin Trillin** writes on social issues, and his forte is his imagination in coming up with good column ideas. Personally, I don't enjoy his writing style as much as the other columnists I've mentioned, but his columns are certainly worth reading.

Trillin, Calvin, *With All Disrespect: More Uncivil Liberties*, New York: Ticknor & Fields, 1985.

- **George F. Will** writes syndicated political and social issue columns, using an elevated style and erudite expression, unlike other columnists such as Royko who tend to write for the common man. Columnist Will is thoroughly entertaining and witty.

Will, George F., *The Morning After/American Successes and Excesses 1981-1986*, New York: The Free Press, 1986.

Will, George F., *Suddenly: The American Idea Abroad and At Home 1986-1990*, New York: The Free Press, 1990.

Selected Reference Books

Following will help you locate where to sell your columns. They are available at your local library:

- *BPI Syndicated Columnist Contacts*, BPI Media Services, PO Box 2015, Lakewood, NJ, 08701.

Lists more than 1,600 major syndicated newspaper columnists and their subject areas. This resource will allow you to find out who's doing what and where.

- *California and Hawaii Publishing Marketplace*. Current Edition. Writers Connection, 1601 Saratoga-Sunnyvale Rd., #180, Cupertino, CA 95014.

Includes listings and descriptions of magazines, newspapers, and newsletters, along with writers' organizations (including local branches) in these states.

- *Editor and Publisher Annual Directory of Syndicated Services Issue*, Editor and Publisher Co., New York.

Lists syndicates serving newspapers in the U.S. and abroad.

- *Editor and Publisher International Yearbook*, Editor and Publisher Co., New York: Current Edition.

Updated annually. Includes listings of daily and weekly U.S. newspapers, listed first by state, then by city, with phone numbers, too. Also gives names of general and departmental editors at these publications, along with circulation figures. In addition, it contains names of syndicates and Canadian papers.

- *Encyclopedia of Associations*, Gale Research Co., Detroit: Current Edition.

Updated annually. Exhaustive multi-volume reference which will help you locate associations, societies, and even fan clubs which have magazines and newsletters to sell your columns to. Or, you can contact these associations for information which you may need to write your column.

- *Gale Directory of Publications and Broadcast Media*, Gale Research, Inc., Detroit: Current Edition.

Updated annually. Includes listings of more than 25,000 newspapers and magazines in the U.S. and their circulation size. Also contains names of departmental editors at newspapers and listings of major syndicates with addresses and phone numbers.

- *Literary Market Place*, R.R. Bowker, New York: Current Edition.

Updated annually. Includes information on syndicates.

- *National Survey of Newspaper "Op-Ed" Pages,* Editor: Marilyn Ross. Communication Creativity, PO Box 909, Buena Vista, CO 81211.

This directory lists leading national newspapers with opinion-editorial pages, offering guest columnists a forum to showcase their views and ideas. It includes information on the editorial needs of each publication along with pay rates and editors' names. It also includes tips on how to best market a message to this medium.

- *Newsletters in Print,* Gale Research Co., Detroit: Current Edition.

Updated annually. Exhaustive directory with newsletters classified by subject area.

- *Oxbridge Directory of Newsletters,* Oxbridge Communications, Inc., New York: Current Edition.

Updated annually. Includes more than 21,000 newsletters in the U.S. and Canada, classified by subject area.

- *Southwest Publishing Marketplace,* Current Edition. Writers Connection, Cupertino, CA.

Includes listings and descriptions of magazines, newspapers, newsletters, and writers' organizations (including local branches) in Nevada, Utah, Arizona, Texas, and Colorado.

- *The Standard Periodical Directory,* Oxbridge Communications, Inc. New York: Current Edition.

Updated annually, this excellent reference is a guide to more than 70,000 U.S. and Canadian magazines, journals, and newsletters. Includes house organs and association publications. The publications are classified by subject area, and you'll find practically every subject imaginable.

- *Ulrich's International Periodicals*, R.R. Bowker Co., New York: Current Edition.

Updated annually. Features about 65,000 magazines and newsletters published throughout the world.

- *Writer's Market*, Writer's Digest Books, Cincinnati: Current Edition.

Updated annually, this includes thousands of listings for magazines, with some newsletters and newspapers. All listings are publications which specifically seek freelance material. Gives details on the type of publication, what kinds of material it seeks, who the target audience of the publication is, what pay is offered, editors' names, among other information. It is also good for its listings of syndicates.

- *Writer's Northwest Handbook*, Current Edition. Media Weavers, 24450 NW Hansen Rd., Hillsboro, OR 97124.

Includes comprehensive listings and descriptions of magazines, newspapers, and newsletters throughout Alaska, British Columbia (Canada), Idaho, Montana, Oregon, and Washington.

Miscellaneous Books

- *The Associated Press Stylebook and Libel Manual*, Edited by Christopher W. French, Addison-Wesley Publishing Co., Inc., Massachusetts:1988.

When you become a seasoned columnist, you might want to look through this style book and pick up abbreviations commonly used by journalists.

- *Beginners' Guide to Writing & Selling Quality Features*, by Charlotte Digregorio, Civetta Press, Oregon: 1990.

Helpful book for those who want to write feature articles and columns alike, as it gives a concise overview of journalism basics.

- *Writer's Friendly Legal Guide*, Edited by Kirk Polking, Writer's Digest Books, Cincinnati: 1989.

Includes advice on syndication contracts, copyright, libel, invasion of privacy, tax deductions, and a variety of other information to help you avoid legal hassles.

General Magazines For Writers

These general writing magazines, which cover a variety of genres, will keep you updated on new markets for your writing, and will also give you tips on the writing craft. In addition, they will keep you abreast of writers' conferences nationally and regionally.

- *Housewife-Writer's Forum.* Deneb Publishing, Lyman, Wyoming. Bi-monthly magazine.

(Incidentally, men read and write for this, too. Men may also get some ideas about writing personal, creative type of columns from this magazine.)

- *New Writer's Magazine.* Sarasota Bay Publishing, Sarasota, Florida. Bi-monthly magazine.

- *The Writer.* The Writer, Inc., Boston. Monthly magazine.

- *Writers' Digest.* F & W Publications, Inc., Cincinnati. Monthly magazine.

Order Form

Please send me ___ copy (ies) of these (softcover) writing books, authored by Charlotte Digregorio and published by Civetta Press:

___ **You Can Be A Columnist: Writing & Selling Your Way To Prestige. ($13.95 each)**

___ **Beginners' Guide to Writing & Selling Quality Features: A Simple Course in Freelancing for Newpapers/Magazines. ($12.95 each)**

Shipping: $2 for one book, plus 75 cents for each additional book.

Your satisfaction is guaranteed.

Name:

Address:

City/State/ZIP:

Phone: (   ) ___ – ___

My check, payable to **Civetta Press,** in the amount of $___ is enclosed.

Please Mail to: Civetta Press, PO Box 1043, Portland, OR 97207-1043, USA.

(Our phone is 503-228-6649.)

Attention Canadians: Orders must be accompanied by a postal money order in U.S. funds.

Quantity Orders Invited

These books are available at special quantity discounts for bulk purchases. For details, contact: Susan Mallory, Special Sales Dept., Civetta Press.

SAN: 200-3171

Notes

Notes